JADE-SKY

CLEAR YOUR OFFICE

*How to cleanse your office and make it a
positive and peaceful environment*

First published in 2016 by New Holland Publishers Pty Ltd
London • Sydney • Auckland

The Chandlery Unit 704, 50 Westminster Bridge Road, London SE1 7QY, United Kingdom
1/66 Gibbes Street, Chatswood, NSW 2067, Australia
5/39 Woodside Ave, Northcote, Auckland 0627, New Zealand

www.newhollandpublishers.com

A record of this book is held at the British Library and the National Library of Australia.

ISBN 9781742576701

Managing Director: Fiona Schultz
Publisher: Diane Ward
Project Editor: Anna Brett
Cover Designer: Andrew Quinlan
Typesetter: Peter Guo
Production Director: Olga Dementiev
Printer: Toppan Leefung Printing Limited

10 9 8 7 6 5 4 3 2 1

Keep up with New Holland Publishers on Facebook
www.facebook.com/NewHollandPublishers

CONTENTS

WHAT IS SPACE CLEARING?

'Space clearing' is a term used to energetically transform a space or area that may have some stagnant, heavy or dull energy attached to it. There are various tools and techniques that can be used to lift the energy in an area to create harmony, balance and to restore the vibrant, positive energy.

Energetic space clearing is not a new concept, it has been around for thousands of years, it is an ancient spiritual technique that is practiced around the world by people from many different religions and cultures. For example, some Indigenous Australian tribes burn eucalyptus leaves and use clap sticks and some Native Americans burn sage, cedar and sweet grass with the use of rattles and drums to space clear an area. In some Asian countries such as China, Thailand, Tibet and Bali they use incense, bells, gongs and chanting to clear a space, whilst in some Western Christian religions church bells, incense, prayers and holy water are used to clear negative energy.

There are many cultures who each have their own unique methods and tools to space clear. It doesn't matter what the differences are amongst the cultures, they all have one thing in common, they all want to clear out the old, negative energy in a space to make it more balanced, positive and protected for the people that live in, work in or visit that space.

CHAPTER ONE

WHEN SHOULD YOU SPACE CLEAR?

Emotional and Physical Signs

Energy is everywhere, it is connected to people, objects, buildings, spaces and environments. Even though you can't see energy with your physical eyes you can definitely feel it physically around you. An example of this is when you walk into a crowded room and you feel the group's energy is stressed or something strange has happened just before you arrived. After you question people about how they are, they admit that earlier in the room there was a fight between two people, this happened just before you arrived. This shows how you can feel energy without seeing it.

Another example that relates to feeling physical energy is when you first meet someone, you may instantly feel unsettled or scared. This is you feeling that person's energy.

Although you intuitively don't feel right about the person, you know that you have to be polite and not judgmental so you may try to ignore that first initial intuitive warning. If you do go against your first gut reaction to the person and later become close to them, you may go on to find out that the person doesn't end up treating you well or that they are dangerous.

Each of us is born with our own unique intuition that allows us to feel warning signs. It also gives us information about what is around us by using our 'sixth sense' to pick up things that our other five senses can't register. Our intuition enables us to pick up on energy around us.

Not all energy is negative, energy can be positive as well. When you space clear an area you want to remove the stagnant, negative energy and replace it with positive, new energy.

There are many different emotional and physical feelings and signs which highlight the need for you to space clear your environment, yourself and your office, they are:

Illness

When someone has been ill or is ill in the office it can affect the emotions and energy of all of the people who work in or visit the office as well energy of the office. It is very important that you take time to clear the energy to get rid of any of the stagnant energy or remnants of feelings or emotions that are a result of the illness.

By space clearing it not only lifts the energy up in the office it also uplifts the people that are in and around the office, it can even help to motivate and uplift the person who is ill and give them a positive energy boost to help them to heal.

STRESS/DEPRESSION

Everyone will experience stress or depression at some stage in their life. It is during these times, or after the stress or depression has occurred, that it is essential that you space clear so that you can recharge, de-stress and reenergise yourself.

Sometimes it is important to have a positive reminder or a routine that gives you comfort in times of stress, by space clearing or having a routine of lighting candles or using oils or incense this can help you to calm down and remember that you will be OK. Some people enjoy looking at the flame of the candle while others relax just by smelling the incense. Some people just need to feel like they are doing something different to switch their current thoughts or mindsets to something positive.

ANGER/FIGHTING

Anger, aggression and fighting all carry such powerful emotions and energy and they leave an energy imprint in the area that they occur in. Have you ever walked into an area and felt really angry suddenly or felt stressed when you were fine a few minutes earlier? If you have you may be intuitively picking up on someone else's angry energy or that area may have a lot of residual energy from past battles, fights or aggressive situations that have occurred there. In that case you are not expected to go and space clear the area that you are visiting or are in but you do need to be mindful of how you are feeling and go and clear your energy before you return home or return to your office.

Try to remove any negative or stressed energy from yourself by consciously remembering it is not your feelings, you are feeling someone else's emotions because you are happy, loved and enjoying yourself. Imagine that you are shining brightly inside and out with gold light, surround yourself in a bubble of gold light, feel all of the negativity disappearing.

It is important that you do clear your own personal energy before returning to your office or home so that you don't bring any negativity with you. Keep your energy positive and bring that positive energy back into your home or work environment.

IF SOMEONE HAS PASSED AWAY

Grief is one of the strongest emotions and it can stick to people energetically, it is a very thick, heavy emotion that can have lasting effects on people physically and emotionally. When someone has passed away in a work place there can be residual energy left behind from the deceased person. It doesn't necessarily have to be a negative energy though because the person may have passed very peacefully or with all of their loved ones around them. It is just that the family members and friends who visit or enter the office or work place have their own grief and emotions attached to that person and their belongings.

It can be very uplifting or helpful if someone does come in and help to space clear the area or smudge (the burning of herbs—see page 46) the area to clear and lift the energy up. By space clearing the work space the family and friends will not feel so heavy or upset when they enter the office.

If someone has passed in a traumatic, violent or unexpected way in a work place or office it is very important that the area is smudged and space cleared to get rid of any of the trapped energy that may be stored there.

FEELING SCARED OR UNEASY

It can be a little bit unsettling to work in an office or work space by yourself when you are not used to it, you may be used to having other people around you or be used to working in a different area. By space clearing you can remove any unsettled or scared energy and this can help you to relax and work better in your work space.

RELATIONSHIP OR BUSINESS PARTNERSHIP BREAK-UPS

Relationship or business partnership break-ups are incredibly painful and hard on all of the people concerned, often people will leave a work place or will spend time away from the work environment due to the relationship or business break-up. It is essential during this unsettling time that you space clear your office and smudge yourself so that you can begin to move forward in your life and in your relationship area.

If there are any items, personal belongings or pieces of furniture that hold any sad memories or past hurts for you it can be helpful if you donate these items to someone in need or try to clear the energy on these items if you do not want to donate them. Remember that each item holds energy from its owners especially jewelry, clothing or anything that is held close to a person's body.

AFTER A ROBBERY OR VANDALISM IN THE WORK PLACE

People can feel like they have been violated after a personal robbery, office invasion or vandalism of their work place. All sense of security and privacy can feel like it has been lost and there can be a fear that this kind of act can happen again.

When someone else's negative energy has entered your work place without your permission or has intruded on your own personal space it is very important that you claim your space back. You can claim your space back by space clearing and setting very strong intentions and reaffirming to yourself that you are safe and protected. It can be helpful to put some extra protection in the work place such as surveillance equipment, security lights and security alarms. This is so that you and the other staff members and any customers or clients can visually see the security devices and it reaffirms to you that you are all OK and are protected.

Signs Around the Work Place

STAGNANT ENERGY

Energy in work environments can become blocked or stagnant and this can happen even if a stressful event hasn't occurred. Just as we should clean our homes to get rid of any dust, dirt or rubbish we must also clean and clear the energy and space around the office or work environment. Even though you can't see the stagnant energy you will be able to feel it. This stagnant energy can feel like a heavy energy which makes you feel tired, depressed or unmotivated. Each room can hold pockets of stagnant energy which need to be cleared so that the positive new energy can come in.

Often you may not notice at first that your office or work place feels stagnant because you are always there you become used to the energy, it isn't until you visit someone else's work place or go on a holiday and stay somewhere else that you realize how different the energy is. How often have you gone on a holiday and thought, wow this hotel or this place feels so amazing? You then return back to work and feel like you are walking back into a heavy energy. This is a big indicator that it is time to space clear your work space.

MOVING INTO A NEW OFFICE OR WORK AREA

It is very exciting to move into a new work space, it is a time of new beginnings and possibilities and with those new beginnings comes positive energy. Before you move into your new work space it is essential that you space clear the whole work area to get rid of any residual energy from the past business owners or staff members, the area and/or any other energy that has attached itself there.

Business/Office Needing to be Sold

If you have had your business on the market for sale for quite some time and it hasn't sold there may be a reason for this, the energy in your work space may need to be cleared. Try to think what has gone on in the building or the office area, have there been any relationship break-ups, illness, death or depression? If you have said yes to any of these things you will definitely have to clear that residual energy out. Even if you can't feel that energy the people looking at your business or office for the first time will feel it.

It is also important to make sure that all owners of the business are ready to sell the business and are equally willing to move and sell. If one of the owners doesn't want to sell it can block the energy or make it harder to sell.

There are many different hints and techniques to help you to sell your office or business faster, I have written about these at the end of this book.

Electrical Items Playing Up

In some work spaces there are constant electrical problems with lights going on and off, light bulbs blowing continuously, printers, laptops, telephones and computers burning out and not working. These electrical problems can seem normal to some people, and they can be straightforward, but what if you have had an electrician out to check your wiring to see what is going on and they can't find any problems at all in your office or work space? This is when you know it is not an electrical problem within the work space, it is an energy problem.

It is important to realize that spirits are made up of energy and they can manipulate the energy to make things happen with electrical items, this doesn't have to be a scary or negative thing it can sometimes be their way of getting your attention to let you know that they are with you.

I know it can be annoying and expensive to have to deal with this so it can be a good idea to space clear the work space to make sure that you get rid of any lower energies or negative energies that may be causing mischief in your business or office. Please note that space clearing won't remove any positive energy or your passed loved ones.

CHAPTER TWO

TYPES OF ENERGY IN THE WORK PLACE/ OFFICE

There are many different types of energies that can be found in your work place; you will have your own energy there as well as the energy of any other people that work with you or visit the work place for business. There are also other energies that can be present in your work place that you may not consciously be aware of, some of these energies are positive and are there to help you, and some of the energies can be negative or a bit mischievous.

It is important that you realize that you do not need to put up with any energy that you do not want there. I will go through some of the different types of energies that you may encounter in your office or work place and it is up to you to decide if you feel like it applies to your work place or not and if you want to space clear and get rid of certain energies.

As I have said earlier please note that you will not be clearing out any positive energies such as your passed loved ones, spirit guides or angels, if you space clear or smudge it will only clear out anything that should not be there or that is negative.

PASSED LOVED ONES

Your passed loved ones are always around you not only when you are at home but also when you are traveling and at work as well, they are guiding you, protecting you and trying to let you know that they are around you. Sometimes you will feel your passed loved ones physically, other times you may receive signs from them or have different things that cannot be explained happen to you, around you and at your home and work place.

An easy way for your passed loved ones to communicate with you or to give you a sign is through the electrical items such as the lights, televisions, radios, ovens, alarm clocks, phones and door bells. Your passed loved ones may turn the electrical items off and on, make them not work, blow the fuse or even put a TV show or song on that you need to watch or listen to.

Please do not be afraid of any of the signs that your passed loved ones send to you, it is just their way to let you know that they are still around you and they still exist. You do not have to smudge to get rid of your passed loved ones, they will go if you ask them to, but if you don't want them to go, they don't need to go.

Original Land or Home Owners

In some offices or work places there is a feeling of being watched or a feeling that you are trespassing on someone else's land, this can be you intuitively picking up on the original home or land owners of the building or work space that you are in. Sometimes a passed spirit is so attached to a space or piece of land they keep coming back there or they are stuck there by their emotional attachment to the place. They can also get caught up in what is going on with the current people that are working there on their old piece of land, the spirit can get confused and think that it is still their home and they can wonder who these people are who are walking around and working on their land or in their building.

Original passed land or home owners do not necessarily go out of their way to cause mischief for the current business owners, they just sometimes get in the way energetically by becoming too involved in the drama and activity within the work place. Often you would see these passed spirits as a shadow, a quick glint of a brightly colored orb of light, or you may feel uneasy like you are being judged or watched by someone.

Residual Energy from Events that have Occurred

There can be residual energy from events that have occurred in a building or work place, usually the residual energy is from traumatic events due to the strong nature of the emotions and energy that comes with trauma.

It can be quite unsettling going into a building or office that has had significant traumatic events happen there. People may feel tense, angry, frustrated or depressed for no particular reason, this is especially true for sensitive, empathetic people. You may not realize why you feel the way you do until you find out the history of the building or what events may have gone on there. This energy can be released and uplifted easily by space clearing and smudging.

SPIRIT GUIDES

Your Spirit Guides are very similar to your passed loved ones, they are here to help you and to protect you. You may feel your Spirit Guides physically in your work place or you may see them out of the corner of your eye as little orbs of white light flickering past.

It is not necessary to space clear to get rid of your Spirit Guides because they are positive spirits who are here to help you. They will not make you feel uneasy or scared, they are very loving and uplifting in their energy.

SPIRITS/GHOSTS—POSITIVE AND NEGATIVE

I don't like the term 'ghosts', I prefer to use the word 'spirits', but I do understand that there is a need to differentiate between the positive and negative spirits. Negative spirits can be called lower entities, ghosts or dark energies they are the mischievous spirits that can make you feel uneasy in your work place, and they can move items around your office or work place, affect the electrical items and make people feel depressed, anxious and stressed.

Normal spirits who are positive spirits are not your passed loved ones, friends or spirit guides they are just spirits who are attracted to your office for some particular reason or they could just be spirits that are passing through that area at the time. These normal positive spirits do not try to scare you or harm you in any way they just are inquisitive and like to see what is going on in your business and your work place.

Traditional Indigenous Land Owners

The traditional indigenous land owners, passed and living, are culturally and spiritually connected to many pieces of land that homes and offices are now built on. Some of this land that homes and offices have been built on carries a lot of ancestral and cultural history with sometimes many thousands of years' worth of rituals and beliefs being embedded into that area. This happens in indigenous areas in countries all around the world.

It is very important that people research and try to find out as much as they can about who originally lived on the land that their business or work place has been built on. If you do find out that it has been used as traditional indigenous land it is a good idea to pay your respects to the traditional indigenous land owner's spirits by acknowledging them and asking them for permission for you and your staff to work there. You can easily do this by smudging the office and asking them in your mind or out loud for their permission, try to let them know that you do acknowledge that it is their land and you do respect them and their culture.

There have been some cases that I have come across where people have not realized that their offices or work spaces have been built on traditional tribal lands. These people couldn't understand why there was so much going wrong in their office with their electrics, their plumbing and with their relationships and business affairs. It was because they had not asked for permission from the traditional indigenous spirits because they were unaware that they should do this. After finding this out and after honoring and respecting the traditional indigenous spirits they found that their electrical, plumbing and relationship problems all began to go away and they could feel happy and at ease in their work place.

ENERGY ATTACHED TO ANTIQUE OR SECOND HAND OBJECTS

It is important that you be mindful of any second hand or antique object that you bring into your office or work place because energy does attach itself to objects. Jewelry and spiritual or religious objects carry a lot of the previous owner's energy which is why you should smudge the items as soon as you bring them into your work place. If you don't smudge the items you may pick up on the energy of the previous owners especially if you are quite intuitive and empathetic and you wear someone else's jewelry.

If you bring a piece of furniture or an item into your office or work place that was previously owned by someone you love that is completely fine because you are bringing happy, loving energy into your office and it is from a person that you know and love. This is a positive thing.

The Boss and the Brewery

A few years ago I was called out to an old mansion that sat on top of a hill in an inner city suburb. This mansion had been converted into a very upmarket office space. The reason I had been called out to this office was some of the staff were being frightened by a spirit or presence in the office. The secretary who called me said she had three staff members who were scared because they had felt, heard or seen something walking around in their boss's office.

I decided to go out to the office to have a look to see if I could help the staff members out. When I left to go to the office I made sure that I took some sage, amethyst crystals, candles and my space clearing spray. On the way to the office I had a feeling that there was a very old male spirit in the office, I was also being shown by my spirit guides the back left hand corner of the building.

When I arrived at the address of the office I noticed that this building was very old, as I walked up to the front door I saw that there was an inscription on a plaque above the door which said 'Built in 1888'. This made sense to me because I did feel that this male spirit was from a long time ago.

The secretary met me at the door to show me around the building. I immediately asked her if I could please see the back left hand corner of the building. I explained to her that was where I was being shown to go. She was quite surprised that I picked that area straight away because that was where her boss's office was and this was also the area in which the staff had experienced a lot of strange things.

When I walked into the boss's office I immediately felt a very strong, old male spirit. I explained this to the secretary and she understood what I was saying, she said to me that she was often scared at night in that room when she had to lock the building up by herself, she felt like she was being watched.

I felt that the old male spirit had owned and lived in this building previously. This office that we were in had an amazing view of the whole of the city, I could sense that the male spirit would often pace back and forth in the room and he would look out at the view of the city.

I let the secretary know what I was feeling, just as I was explaining it to her another staff member walked in, he was a young male and he was interested to find out what was going on and why I was there in the boss's office. He listened to what I had to say, then he told me what he had personally experienced. He told me that he often worked alone at night and on the weekends in the office directly underneath the boss's office, while he is working sometimes he hears heavy footsteps and chairs being moved around upstairs above his office. He said that he has come immediately upstairs to check who is in the office and he has been surprised to find out that no one is there. This has left him frightened on many occasions.

This young man went on to tell me that the original owner of the mansion had also owned the big old brewery in the city which could be seen from the office window. This made sense to me because the male spirit was so attached to his home and brewery he was stuck, he hadn't moved on to the light or gone into the spirit world. This male spirit was scaring the staff members, particularly the female staff because he couldn't understand why females were in his home. He didn't mind the people in his home during working hours but after hours he would get angry and frustrated because he wanted to be left alone.

After explaining all of this to the secretary I asked her if she could contact her boss to see what he wanted to do with this situation and to ask if it was OK for me to help this male spirit to go to the light and move on. She said of course she would contact him straight away.

When the secretary came back to let me know that it was OK, she was concerned that whatever we did to help the male spirit may hurt him in some way. I explained to her that we wouldn't hurt him, it would just help him to move on spiritually so he wasn't trapped or stuck energetically anymore.

After getting permission from the secretary and her boss the first thing I did was put down a crystal protection grid in the boss's office. I did this by using the four amethyst crystal points that I had brought with me. I placed one amethyst point in each of the four corners of the room. This was to form the grid to provide protection for the room.

I then sprayed my protection space clearing spray into each of the four corners of the room. As I sprayed I said out loud

"I now remove all negativity from this room". This was to clear out the stagnant energy and to calm the male spirit's energy down. After doing this I let the secretary know that I would wait and see how the office went in the next few days, to see if they were happy to leave it as is, or if they were still experiencing things they could call me and I would come back and clear the spirit out for good when the boss was available to be there. She agreed to this.

A few days later the secretary called me to say that the boss was back and he wanted me to come back to the office, he was worried about his staff members. I agreed to go back. When I arrived the boss was happy to meet me, he wanted to clear the energy out of his office. We immediately went to his office and disconnected all of the electrical devices. I then asked the boss to walk around the room with me so that he could spray the space clearing and protection spray and reaffirm what I had said earlier in the week, "I now remove all negativity from this room" and I asked him to also add "I release you in love and light, so that you can return to spirit world".

After the boss sprayed the room and reaffirmed what he wanted I called the secretary and another female staff member into the room. I instructed the boss and the female staff members to hold hands with each other and with me to form a circle. I lit three white candles first, then a purple candle and placed it in front of us in the middle of the circle. I explained to them it may get hot in the room, and not to be afraid and to keep the circle intact.

I then said out loud to the spirit it was time for him to move on now, he was no longer needed in this office, they would all be OK. I also told him that there were far more important and wonderful things waiting for him in the spirit world.

The male spirit was stubborn and resisting moving on so I asked the boss to repeat his earlier words three times "I release you in love and light." The male spirit said to me to tell the boss of the office he needed to reconnect with his friend and he mentioned a name. He then said to the boss to remember to not become too much of a loner, like he had became.

As soon as I passed the message on to the boss I felt the male spirit's energy shift, he became lighter. As the male spirit started to leave he asked me to tell the boss a final message—"family always comes first and never forget that! Don't be alone!"

I thanked the spirit and so did the boss, the boss also said he wouldn't forget his message. I saw and felt the male spirit leave. Sometimes all it takes for a spirit to move on is a little encouragement or for them to tie up some loose emotional ends.

After I explained to the boss and his two staff members what I had seen and felt, we all let out a sigh of relief and stopped holding each other's hands and I snuffed the candles out. It's very important not to blow candles out as it causes the energy to scatter. If you snuff the candles out the energy is contained. The room instantly felt lighter.

I left the building and a few days later I checked back in with the secretary. She said they all were relieved and happy and hadn't felt the male spirit's energy again.

TOOLS AND TECHNIQUES TO SPACE CLEAR

Crystals

CRYSTALS USED IN SPACE CLEARING

Crystals are wonderful natural healers from the mineral kingdom—they are full of positive energy and they can help you to clear the energy of a space instantly. Each crystal has its own unique healing property and energy, you can use a crystal by itself, hang a crystal from a window or ceiling or choose to put multiple crystals together that resonate with you. You may even like to wear a crystal as a talisman or have a crystal in your pocket, there are so many different ways to harness the positive energy of crystals.

CLEANSING YOUR CRYSTALS

It is important that you cleanse your crystals when you first bring them into your office or work place. This is important so that you can remove any old energies, or memories which may have been stored inside the crystal.

To cleanse your crystal you can use any of the following methods:

△ *Leave the crystals out in the direct sunlight for a day or longer*

△ *Put the crystals out in the full moon*

△ *Place the crystals into the earth, with their point facing up for approx. two to three days*

△ *Use incense or smudge sticks and wave the smoke over all sides of the crystal*

△ *Put the crystal in sea water or rock salt water*

△ *Place the crystal on the sand at the beach*

△ *Visualize and put good intent into the crystal asking for all negative energy to be removed*

Once you have cleansed your crystals you then can begin to place the crystals around your work place to help lift the energy and keep the work place a positive space where people enjoy working, visiting and spending time.

USING CRYSTALS TO UPLIFT AND REMOVE NEGATIVE/ STAGNANT ENERGY IN THE OFFICE OR WORK PLACE

Place crystal clusters such as amethyst or citrine in and around your work place, you may even like to have bowls of crystals on your window sills, on top of a fire place, bookcase or even have a crystal cluster or bowl of crystals in the middle of a table in the staff kitchen or in the reception room of your business.

The following crystals work very well together and are great for clearing energy in your work place:

Amethyst
Color: Purple

Healing Properties: Helps to calm and protect you. Removes negativity and helps to overcome fears and reoccurring nightmares. It enhances spiritual awareness.

An amethyst gets rid of anger, anxiety and helps to balance out emotions of loss and grief.

An amethyst cluster (a crystal made up with many smaller crystals) can be placed in any room of your office or work place to clear any unwanted energies and to calm people down. You can also place amethyst on top of your air conditioners, computers, printers and television sets to reduce the radiation and electrical smog in your work place.

Aventurine
Color: Green (also comes in brown, red, blue and peach)

Healing Properties: Aventurine is a great crystal for courage; it also helps you to feel happy and positive. This crystal will help you feel creative, confident and strong. It will help your heart and lungs.

Place an aventurine in your pocket when you are starting a new job, new business, new class or sport and it will give you a confidence boost. Place a piece of aventurine by itself or with other crystals in the main meeting or conference room and the staff room/kitchen.

Black Obsidian
Color: Black

Healing Properties: Black Obsidian is a very powerful crystal that can help to disperse any negative energy that is around you personally or that is in your work place. This crystal calms the energy down in a work environment and helps to keep the business free of negativity.

You can place a piece of black obsidian in the front and back door area of your office or work place to provide extra protection, or you can place it on your own personal desk at work to help you to feel safe, secure and calm. If you feel frightened or nervous hold a piece of black obsidian in the palm of your hand.

Black Tourmaline
Color: Black

Healing Properties: Black tourmaline is very similar in its healing properties to black obsidian. It is a crystal that gets rid of negative energies so that positive energy, wellbeing and prosperity can come in. By getting rid of the negative energies black tourmaline improves the energy and vibration of the air where it is located.

You may like to wear a piece of black tourmaline in jewelry or carry a piece in your pocket. In the work place it is a good idea to keep black tourmaline in a drawer in your desk or on top of your desk because it will space clear and protect the room that you work in. For extra protection you may even like to put or hang a piece of black tourmaline at the front and back door of your work place if you can.

Carnelian
Color: Orange (also comes in red, pink and brown)
Healing Properties: Carnelian is a great crystal for feeling confident and for helping you feel secure in your life.

This crystal helps you to trust in yourself and your gifts and helps you to overcome fears. It also calms anger down.

Place a carnelian crystal in your pocket or in a crystal pouch to help calm you, or have a piece of carnelian in your office/ work place or on your desk to give you a boost of confidence and positivity.

Citrine
Color: Bright Yellow and Orange
Healing Properties: This is a crystal which holds no negativity it is one of the only crystals that you do not need to cleanse. It brings positivity and abundance into your work place, business and your life.

Place a piece of citrine or a citrine cluster in the back left hand corner of your office or work place to increase your wealth because this is your wealth corner according to Feng Shui. Citrine is known as the wealth stone so if you have a cash box, cash register or safe in your office place a piece of citrine in there (put it in the back left hand section) to increase the wealth of the business.

Clear Quartz
Color: Clear

Healing Properties: Clear quartz is a fantastic general all-purpose healing crystal, it helps with concentration and removes negativity.

Clear quartz helps your immune system, it brings balance to your body and helps you to think more clearly. It also helps enhance psychic abilities and meditation.

Hematite
Color: Silver/Metallic Gray

Healing Properties: Hematite is a very grounding and protective crystal it makes us feel safe and secure and rebalances us. It is the stone of the mind so it can help you to concentrate, think and focus on what you need to do.

Hematite can also prevent you from absorbing any negative energy from other people or places, which is why it is an important and powerful crystal to have in your work environment. You can place this crystal anywhere in your work place. Hematite is also great if you have migraines or headaches, you just need to place a piece of hematite on your forehead or behind your ears and you will feel your headache go away.

Red Jasper
Color: Red/Maroon

Healing Properties: Red Jasper is a protective crystal, it helps to ground your energy and guard you against physical threats. It is also a great crystal to stimulate passion in your personal and work life and it helps you to get creative, to manifest new ideas and move forwards towards new beginnings in your life.

You can wear red jasper in a pendant, bracelet or keep a piece in your pocket, or you may like to place a piece of red jasper in your office or work area to absorb any negativity and radiation. You can also keep red jasper in your car to prevent road rage, theft or car accidents.

Rose Quartz
Color: Pink

Healing Properties: Rose quartz is a very loving soothing crystal which helps heal broken hearts and hurt feelings. It calms and gets rid of fears, anxiety and hyperactivity.

This crystal helps you to build self-confidence, self-trust and encourages love, compassion and understanding. Wear a rose quartz pendant over your heart to feel loved and confident.

Smokey Quartz
Color: Gray, Brown and Black

Healing Properties: Smokey quartz is an excellent crystal for relieving stress, fear or any other negative emotions. Smokey quartz transforms the dense negative energy into positive energy, it is a very helpful stone to have in the work place because it is very calming and it encourages inner strength and serenity.

Place a piece of smokey quartz in your home office or workplace to enhance organizational skills.

Tiger Eye
Color: Gold and Brown
Healing Properties: Tiger Eye is fantastic to help you ground your energy and feel more stable in your life. It helps you to organize yourself and feel confident in times of change.

This crystal helps you to feel secure in your surroundings and calms anger down. It also helps you to become more creative and focused, so it is great for new beginnings in the work place, new business ideas or jobs.

FENG SHUI PLACEMENT OF CRYSTALS IN YOUR OFFICE OR WORK PLACE

According to the ancient art of Feng Shui if you place particular crystals in strategic places around your office or work place it can have positive effects on all aspects of yours and the other staff member's lives.

Please see the diagram below to find out about each area of the office and work place and how it relates to different parts of your life. The diagram will also give you an example of which crystals to use in each separate place in your office.

You may choose to just place a crystal in one area that you want to focus on, or you may like to put a crystal in each area, it is totally up to you what you decide to do. Remember as I have said earlier you must cleanse your crystals first before you use them.

Feng Shui Bagua Chart

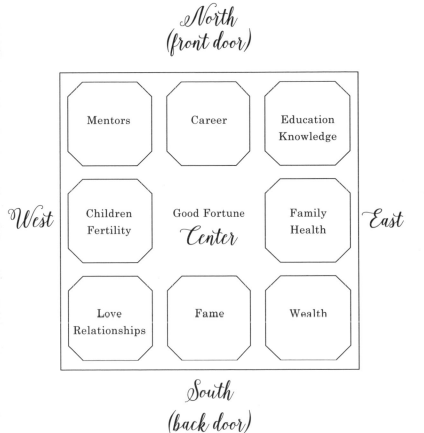

Crystals to use in each area of the office

Northwest = Mentor Corner *(Color: Purple/ Gray)*

Place an amethyst cluster or crystal in the northwest corner of your office to encourage positive support from mentors, helpful people and the Universe.

North = Career Area *(Color: Dark Blue/Black)*

Place a sodalite or lapis lazuli crystal in the northern area of your office to enhance your intuition and to help you to make the right career decisions.

Northeast = Education and Knowledge Corner *(Color: Blue/Green)*

Place a piece of turquoise in the northeast corner of your office for balance, positive energy, wisdom, self-knowledge and wonderful educational opportunities.

Southwest = Love and Relationships Corner *(Color: Pink/ Skin Earth Tones)*

Place a large piece of rose quartz cluster in the southwest corner of your office to encourage or attract a wonderful long lasting, equal, loving relationship.

South = Fame Area *(Color: Red)*

Place or hang a large red jasper crystal in the southern area of your office to enhance your recognition and fame and to improve your career prospects.

Southeast = Wealth Corner *(Color: Purple/Green/Gold)*

Place a cluster of citrine in the southeast corner of your office to bring wealth and prosperity to you and those in your business.

East = Family and Health *(Color: Purple/Green/Gold)*

Place a jade crystal in the eastern area of your office to promote good health, long life, wealth and happiness for you and your staff.

West = Children and Fertility *(Color: White/Pastel colors)*

Place a piece of rainbow moonstone in the western area of your office to increase your fertility and to also bring positive energy to any children in your family.

Center of Office = Good Fortune *(Color: Yellow/Earth Tones)*

Place a piece of citrine in the center of your office to increase the abundance and good fortune in your life. Citrine's positive energy will uplift all members of your household.

You can place a single crystal in each of the areas above because all of the crystals are excellent space clearers, however you don't need to just wear the crystals as a talisman or place them individually around your office, you can place your crystals in specific geometric patterns which are called crystal grids.

People use crystal grids to clear the space in their office or to bring a specific intention or energy into their business and work place. When you use a crystal grid and add your energy and intentions it can often be more powerful than using a single crystal for an intended goal.

Crystal Gridding

WHAT IS CRYSTAL GRIDDING?

As I have discussed earlier crystals are great for space clearing an area, they can be used to change and enhance the vibrations of a home or office or even outdoor areas, such as gardens, pool areas or ley lines.

To create a crystal grid you need to place specific crystals in strategic positions and locations within the space where you want to enhance or amplify the energy. Crystals are natural energy amplifiers, they are fantastic at creating positive uplifting energy in a space. To make a crystal grid you need to have more than one crystal because each crystal needs to link together in a network, you can use as many crystals as you want there is no limit.

There are many different patterns that you can create when you make a crystal grid, usually the patterns are in a geometric pattern with one crystal in the center of the grid being the master crystal. Each grid has its own special purpose and is unique so you do not have to follow any strict rules to what you do with your crystal grid, there is no right or wrong way to create a crystal grid, the most important thing to do is to have the right intention when you make the grid and to also use crystals that have been cleansed.

How do you create a crystal grid?

It isn't hard to create a crystal grid, you can create a simple crystal grid that protects your work space or office just by using five crystals of your choice, I like to use black onyx, black obsidian or amethyst for this kind of grid because of their protective energy. I also like to use crystals that have one natural point on the end if they are available. If you don't have natural points it is better to use tumbled crystals.

Tumbled crystals are natural crystals which have been polished or machine tumbled to make the surface of the crystal smooth to touch, it also gives the crystal a nice polished shine. Tumbled crystals are easy to hold in your hand and are not rough like natural crystals which may have sharp or rough edges or surfaces. Many people prefer to use tumbled crystals because they can wear them against their body without the edges scratching them. They are also sometimes referred to as tumbled stones.

Once you decide on the crystals that you want to use, you have to decide on the intent that you want to put into your crystal grid i.e. what is it that you want this crystal grid to achieve for you?

A Simple Five Crystal Pyramid Protection Grid for the Office

After you have decided on your intent begin to place one crystal in each corner of your office or room that you want to protect. Leave one crystal to be the master crystal or center crystal in the middle of your office (or as close as possible to the middle of the office) or room. For the master/center crystal I usually like to use a clear quartz because they are fantastic amplifiers.

The master crystal is responsible for communicating with the other four crystals to help keep the energy going in harmony. You can also do this crystal grid with just four crystals, with one in each corner but it is not as powerful as using the five crystals. When you use the five crystals you are harnessing the energy of the fifth crystal and by placing it in the center of the office or room it creates an amazing pyramid shape which is very powerful.

Here is an example of intention that you can say when you lay your protection grid down in your office. (Please note that you can add your own religious, spiritual or beliefs to this and create your own unique prayer or mantra that will serve you best.)

Prayer/mantra/intention for protection for yourself and the business

Please... bless and protect this person/people that stands before you *(say all the names of your staff here)* and all the people who will come to work or visit here in the future with my/our blessing. Please bring good health, abundance, happiness and love to this business.

Please... clear and cleanse this office of any negativity or stagnant energy that resides here and use my intention and these crystals to do this. Free this office of any and all that would do harm to any of us and protect us from any outsiders that would do us harm of any kind, for the good of all and harm to none.

We honor the traditional owners of this land both past and present with respect and thank them for having us on their land.

Thank you... We are grateful for everything that you help us with and provide us with each and every day.

Here is an example of the five crystal protection grid layout for your office:

Five crystal pyramid protection grid for the office

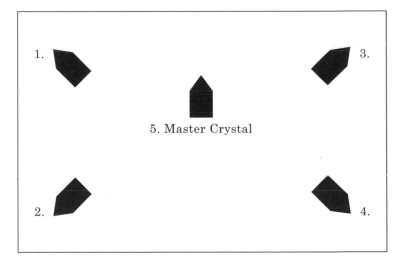

Protection grid for the property including the outside areas

You can also make and use this crystal grid on a larger scale by placing one crystal in each corner outside of your office in your yard. Bury a crystal in each corner of your yard, state your intention and place the master crystal inside in the middle of your office. This will create an even larger protective energy for your office environment.

Prayer/mantra/intention for protection for the complete property/office

Please... bless, clear, protect and cleanse this land of any negativity that resides here and use my intention and these crystals to do this. Please free this land of any negativity, stagnant energy and all that would do harm to any of us. Protect us from any outsiders that would do us harm of any kind, for the good of all and harm to none.

We honor the traditional owners of this land both past and present with respect and thank them for having us on their land.

Thank you... We are grateful for everything that you help us with and provide us with each and every day.

Protection grid for the property including the outside areas

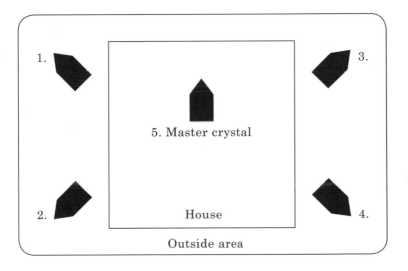

CRYSTAL GRIDDING ON A SMALLER SCALE

Crystal grids work on a smaller scale as well, you do not need to create a grid that covers your whole office you may like to create a smaller grid with a specific intent that you can have in your staff room, meeting room or reception area. You can place your crystal grid on a table, up on top of a bookshelf or even on top of a filing cabinet, it doesn't really matter where you place it as long as you know it is safe and out of the reach of young children.

You can leave your crystal grid in place for as long as you want or need it, you should try to cleanse the crystals on a regular basis or when you feel like you need to.

Here is a suggestion of an abundance and prosperity grid that you may like to use in your office:

Abundance and prosperity grid

For this abundance and prosperity grid focus on what you would like to achieve and how you would like to have abundance and prosperity enter your life. Select the crystals that you would like to use or that resonate with you the most. I personally would use a big citrine cluster or piece of citrine, a large piece of aventurine as well as some clear quartz points, some jade, red jasper and any other crystals that you feel drawn to.

The best place to put this abundance and prosperity grid is in the back left hand corner of your office in your wealth corner or next to your computer, in your office or wherever you spend a lot of time working.

You can make this grid in any way that you feel drawn to, please see an example below of how I would usually make my abundance and prosperity crystal grid:

Abundance and prosperity grid

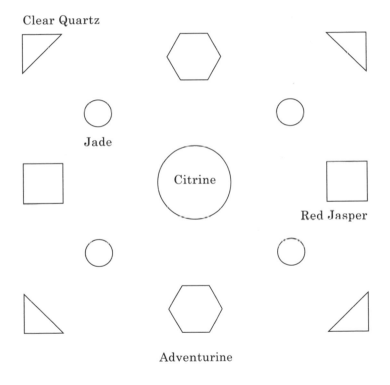

Intent

Just remember the most important thing about crystal gridding and space clearing is the intent that you put behind it, make sure you are clear about what your intent in and stick to it.

Smudging and Smudge Sticks

SMUDGING

Smudging is an ancient ritual which involves burning specific herbs to clear out and get rid of any negative energies or entities. The burning herbs create a protective smoke around a person, object or a place. The traditional herbs used in Native American smudging ceremonies are cedar, sweet grass and sage. The herbs can be bound together with thread or string to form a smudge stick or they can be placed in an abalone shell, which needs to have sand or soil in it to prevent it from overheating, or you can use a heat resistant bowl.

The word smudging traditionally comes from the Native American culture however there are many different cultures around the world who have their own type of ritual or smudging ceremony. The indigenous Australians are an example of this because they have their own form of a smudging ceremony called a smoking ceremony. In the smoking ceremony various native plants such as eucalyptus leaves are burnt, sometimes on top of a large piece of bark off a tree.

It is not only indigenous cultures that use smoke or smudging to clear out negative energies, many different religions have their own ceremonies to purify and protect a person or place. An example of this is during religious ceremonies in the Catholic Church the priest will use incense and frankincense to clear the energy and protect the church and all who are in it.

Smudging ceremonies focus on bringing balance to all aspects of a person: physically, spiritually and mentally, they are also used to create balance in the office and the environment.

The intent behind the smudging is just as important as the actual smudging herbs. It is very important that you smudge when you are ready to clear out any old, negative or stale energy in and around your office. Smudging is also a great self-care activity to keep your energy positive, uplifted and recharged.

HOW TO SMUDGE YOUR WORK PLACE

The first thing that you should do before you begin to smudge your work place is to have a clear intent about what you want to achieve by smudging. I would say that most people would have a similar intent for their work place i.e. they would like their work place and all of the people in it to be safe, protected, and healthy and for all that visit or live there to feel uplifted, happy and relaxed inside that space. You may have a different intent, just make sure you are clear.

Equipment needed to smudge your work place

You will have to have the right equipment to smudge your work place, you can use anything that you like but for a traditional Native American smudging ceremony there are a few things that you will need, they are as follows:

Δ *Herbs such as sage, cedar or sweet grass either in loose leaf form or tied into a smudge stick*
  * *sage—is used to get rid of negative energy and to keep negative energy out*
  * *cedar—is used to purify a space*
  * *sweet grass—is used to bring in good energy*
Δ *Matches or a lighter*
Δ *An abalone or paua shell, or a heat resistant bowl*
Δ *Dirt or sand to put in the shell or bowl*
Δ *A large feather or feather prayer fan (this is optional, you can also use your hand)*

Once you have all of these things you are ready to begin to smudge yourself and your work place. Try to get permission from the boss or owner of the work place to make sure that it is OK for you to smudge there. You may need to smudge after hours when the work place is closed so that you can make sure that you will not be disturbed during the smudging process because you will need to focus on your intent.

Step one: Place a small amount of sand or dirt in the shell or bowl, then place your loose herbs on top and light them with the matches or a lighter and gently blow on them.

If you have a smudge stick you do not need to use the bowl

or shell however you can use it to catch any of the herbs which fall off. Light the smudge stick with matches or a lighter and gently blow on it to get it smoking. If the fire goes out just relight it as needed. Remember to be aware of any smoke detectors in your office because some smoke detectors can be set off by the sage smoke.

Step two: Start smudging in the most northerly part of your office, walk with the lit herbs in the smoking shell/bowl or smudge stick in a clockwise direction, starting from the north. Fan the smoke with your feather or hand and think of your intent, or state it out loud, and ask for all negativity to be removed. Make sure that you fan the smoke into all corners of every room in the office, even behind doors.

Step three: As you walk around the whole office in a clockwise direction you should eventually end up back at your original starting point. Once you have smudged your office you can smudge yourself by fanning the smoke over your face and body with the feather or your hand to purify yourself.

Step four: When you have finished with the smudging herbs it is important to snuff the smudge stick or loose herbs out in the sand or dirt. If possible bury the old sand or dirt with the loose herbs in it outside under a tree. If you can't do this just dispose of it thoughtfully.

Note: *Smudge sticks can be used more than once depending on their size.*

Step five: After smudging your office and yourself it is important that you open up all of the curtains/blinds and windows in your office (if possible) to let all of the old negative energy out.

Please note that it is important that you do not smudge in small enclosed areas if you are pregnant, have babies or small children around you, or are asthmatic. If any of these things apply to you, you may like to use an incense stick or an aromatherapy spritzer spray instead, they are just as powerful, remember it is the intent that accompanies them that really makes a difference.

INCENSE

Incense has been used in its basic form since the beginning of human history to clear energy and change the emotions of the people who are around it. Our ancestors realized that some herbs, plants and spices emit distinctive and sometimes very potent scents when burnt.

Most cultures throughout history have used sacred herbs, plants and spices for their rituals and ceremonies and for specific healing purposes. The scents that are produced by the various herbs, plants and spices would help to clear, disinfect and purify the energy around the office and work environment as well as change the mood of the people and heighten their senses.

You can still use incense today in modern times to clear out any negativity, cleanse your office or work space, and to relax your mind and body. There are many different types of incense available to purchase, try different varieties of incense and if you find one that suits you and you enjoy its scent you can regularly use it to clear the energy in and around your office.

The following list highlights what each incense is, and what it is used for. Please note that there are many different types of incense around and many different belief systems connected to them.

INCENSE	USAGE
Bamboo	Luck and Protection
Cedar	Purification, Protection and Release
Champa	Harmony, Clearing and Protection
Desert Sage	Purification, Wisdom and Protection
Eucalyptus Leaf	Healing and Protection
Frankincense	Purification and Spiritual Growth
Jasmine Flowers	Relaxation and Sleep
Lavender	Clear and Cleanse
Lilac	Peace, Harmony and Protection
Nag Champa	Cleanse and Clear
Pine Needles/Cones	Protection and Health
Rose Petals	Love, Success and Protection
Rosemary	Concentration and Memory
Sage	Protection and Clearing
Sweet Grass	Purification and Clearing

How to Space Clear with Incense

To space clear or smudge your office or work space with incense you use a similar procedure as the smudging ceremony.

Step one: Decide on your intent and choose which incense you would like to use. Try to use incense that you like the smell of otherwise it can be counterproductive if you are trying to clear out negativity and you don't feel positive about the smell.

Step two: Start by lighting the incense in the most northern part of your office, walk with the lit incense in a clockwise direction, starting from the north. Fan the smoke from the incense with your hand and think of your intent or state it out loud and ask for all negativity to be removed. Make sure that you fan the smoke into all of the corners of every room in the office, even behind doors.

Step three: As you walk around the whole office in a clockwise direction you should eventually end up back at your original starting point. Once you have cleared the energy in your office you can clear the energy around yourself by fanning the incense smoke over your face and body with your hand to purify yourself.

Step four: When you have finished with the incense stick it is important to snuff it out or let it continue to burn in an incense holder.

Step five: After space clearing your office and yourself it is important that you open up all of the curtains/blinds and windows in your office (if possible) to let all of the old negative energy out.

ESSENTIAL OILS

Essential Oils are great for people to use in their work environment if they do not want to use smudge sticks, incense or herbs due to the smells and smoke that they create. Essential Oils are also great to use to keep the energy positive around the work place as they smell fantastic.

HOW TO USE ESSENTIAL OILS TO CLEAR THE ENERGY IN YOUR WORK PLACE

There are various different ways that you can use essential oils to space clear your work place, you can use an oil burner, a diffuser or a spritzer/spray bottle that you can add distilled water to and spray it around your office or work space.

It is very important that you try to use only quality essential oils not the cheaper aromatherapy or fragrance oils for the best possible space clearing energy. The reason that I suggest using essential oils is because essential oils contain therapeutic benefits whereas fragrance oils smell nice but do not contain the same healing properties as essential oils.

Here is a list of essential oils that can be used in your office for space clearing:

Please note that some essential oils are not appropriate for use during pregnancy, or if you have epilepsy or certain allergies and sensitivities, research or ask your Doctor or Naturopath about the essential oils you are using if you have any of these conditions.

ESSENTIAL OIL	USAGE
Bergamot	Balancing and Uplifting
Frankincense	Mental Strength, Peace, Purification
Geranium	Release, Calm and Clarity
Jasmine	Self Confidence and Optimism
Lavender	Cleansing, Detoxifying and Balance
Myrrh	Clarity, Focus and Strength
Peppermint	Cleansing and Detoxifying
Rose	Love and Peace

SEA SALT

Using natural sea salt is a very powerful, safe and effective way to space clear and lift the energy in your work environment. You can buy ready-made sea salt or you can make your own by evaporating seawater so that only the salt remains. I prefer using natural sea salt instead of using normal household processed table salt.

How to use sea salt to space clear your office or work space

To cleanse and space clear an office or work space with sea salt you can place small amounts of sea salt in bowls and place them in the four corners of your office or four corners of the space that you wish to space clear. When you are placing the bowls down it is important that you state your intention that you wish to clear out any negativity energy from the space. It is up to you how long you want to leave the salt bowls out, I would usually leave the bowls out for around one to two days. When you are finished with the salt in the bowls try to bury the salt in the ground outside or throw it immediately into a bag and place it into a bin, do not reuse the salt because it will contain all the impurities and negativity energy.

If you don't want to leave sea salt out in bowls you can easily make a sea salt spritzer that you can spray in and around the office or work space. To make your own sea salt spritzer dissolve two teaspoons of sea salt into some clean warm water and pour it into a spray bottle, you can use this whenever you need to.

Chapter Three

CANDLES

Candles are an everyday item that many people have in their home or office, they may have decorative candles, emergency candles for use in the case of power outages, birthday cake candles or scented candles. It doesn't matter what type of candle it is, each candle has a specific purpose and that purpose is to bring light into an area, to get rid of the darkness.

Candles can also be used for space clearing and to set positive intentions into a space. Setting an intention or making a wish is just like when you were a young child, you would make a wish before you blew out your birthday candles. Now as an adult you can make a wish or set an intention in your office. You may choose to light the candle because it smells nice and it relaxes you or you may like to light the candle and set an intention.

There are many different types of candles that you can use it is personal preference which you choose. I am not too concerned by the size or shape of the candles that I use because I feel it is more important to focus on your intention and what you want to achieve by lighting the candle.

Just as there are many different kinds of candles there are also many different colors of candles that you can use. It is important to know that each color does represent a different healing property and energy. Try to decide what it is that you want achieve by lighting the candle i.e. what is your intention, once you decide your intention you can choose a candle in the color that matches that intention.

When you have an intention and match that intention to a specific color which has those healing properties or energies you can increase the power and energy behind your intention.

You can even take it a step further and try to get a candle that has essential oils added to it so you can have the color of the candle that you want, the essential oil that you need and then all you need to do is add your intention to it.

Here is a list of colors that I relate to specific healing properties and energies, you may have your own ideas about what colors relate to different things for you, always go by what feels right for you, this is just a guide:

COLOR	HEALING PROPERTIES OR ENERGY
Yellow	Positivity, Abundance, Creativity
Red	Affection, Love, Passion
Pink	Compassion, Love, Relationships
Light Blue	Peace, Relaxation, Harmony
Dark Blue	Protection, Intuition
Green	Healing, Clearing, Good Fortune
Purple	Protection, Spiritual Connections
White	Purity, Clarity, Peace

How to use your candle to space clear your office

Once you have decided on your intention and you have the candle of your choice it is quite easy to set your intention with the use of a candle.

The first thing you need to do is make sure that the candle is safe in a small glass bowl, a candle holder or on a dish so that you don't burn yourself. When you are ready it is important that you focus on your intention for example you may ask in your mind that you and everyone that works or visits your office will be safe, healthy and protected.

As soon as you feel you have your intention light your candle, I would then focus on walking from the northern part of your office and go into every room of your office, just as you would do if you were smudging your office with herbs or incense. Make sure that you have the candle lit throughout the whole process and that you are thinking of your intention or saying it out loud as you walk around.

Keep walking around the office in a clockwise direction until you end up back at the beginning, where you started. It is important that you do not blow your candle out when you are finished, you may choose to leave the candle burning (with supervision of course) or you can safely snuff your candle out with the bottom of a tea cup or with a candle snuffer. The reason you should not blow the candle out is because it blows out the intentions and disperses all the strong energy that you have just created.

If you still have some of your candle left and it has not melted completely it is important that you do not use this candle again for any other purpose, it has its own special intention so it will not be able to be used again. It is best to keep these candles separate from any other candles that you may have in your office.

You may like to repeat this process whenever you feel that you need to pick the energy up in your office or if you would like to put an intention out for a specific healing energy you can focus on a specific room in your office for example if you were looking for new creative ideas for the business you would focus on a yellow candle and have it lit in your career area (see the Feng Shui Bagua Chart in the crystals section for more details).

Words of Affirmations

Words are very powerful things, they can make or break you, which is why it is so important to think before you speak. Just as people can be affected by what other people say around them so can the energy of your work place. Try to be mindful of what you say in your work place, it is important that you infuse your work environment with loving, positive thoughts, energy and words.

Each time you use positive words of affirmations in your work place you are lifting the energy in your work and business life. People who come to visit your work place may wonder why they feel so happy to be in your space and you may notice that they don't want to rush off or leave.

To remind yourself of positive affirmations or prayers you could write down some and attach them to the staffroom fridge or hang inspirational sayings on prints on the wall or note them down in a calendar in your office. It doesn't matter if you have these up on your wall or not it just matters that you are consciously trying to put positive thoughts out into your work place.

You may like to write your own positive affirmations, or you can use some of these examples:

Δ *My work place and all who work and visit here are safe, loved and protected*

Δ *Only positive energies are allowed into this office, all other energies will not enter*

Δ *I am blessed and so are all that enter my office*

Δ *I am thankful for my business and thankful for everyone and everything in it*

Δ *All of my family, friends and myself are happy and healthy as is my home and work place*

Δ *Abundance comes in all forms to myself, my colleagues and my friends instantly for the good of all and harm to none*

CLEARING SPACE WITH SOUND: CLAPPING, BELLS, DRUMS AND SINGING BOWLS

People can be affected both emotionally and physically by sounds, even if the sound is not heard its vibrations can be felt. Some sounds are very healing such as music, chimes, singing bowls and drums. You can use sounds to not only uplift and heal yourself but also to space clear your work environment. A great thing about using sound to space clear is that it is not messy, it doesn't have to make any smells and there is no risk of the smoke alarm going off.

When you space clear your work space you can use many different types of sounds, for example you may like to sing, clap your hands, use a musical instrument or even turn the radio on or play a CD. It doesn't matter what sound or instrument you use to make the sound, it is the intent behind making the sound that is the most important thing.

Everyone is an individual so it is totally up to you what you use to space clear your work space with, there are a various different tools or instruments you can use, you may choose to use just one or you may like to use a variety of different tools. Just make sure that everyone else that shares your work place is OK with the kinds of sound you are using, if it doesn't suit everyone it can cause negative energy instead of positive energy. You may need to space clear with sound after hours when all of the other customers and staff members have left the work area.

I have listed a few examples of the more common instruments and tools below, try and find which ones you are drawn to or what feels right for you.

Clapping

Clapping is a very easy and effective tool to disperse any negative or stagnant energy in a room or work space. It is important that you use loud, purposeful clapping with a positive intention in your mind that you would like to clear the space and only have positive energy remain.

How to space clear with clapping

△ *Make sure you take a deep breath in, then breathe out, get your body relaxed. When you are ready set your intention in your mind or state it out loud for example you may say "I remove all negativity from this space, only positive energy remains".*

△ *Begin by using small quick claps, listen to hear what the sound is like, does it sound like a dull clap or a crisp clap? As you start clapping work your way up from small fast claps to bigger louder claps.*

△ *To uplift the energy in the space it is a good idea to start clapping from the middle of the room and into each corner of the room. You will notice the difference in the sound of the clapping, when a space is clear and full of positive energy the sound will be clear and crisp not dull.*

△ *When you feel you are finished shake your hands around in front of you at least three times and imagine that you are clean from head to toe and filled with clear, bright white light.*

Bells

Bells have been used by various different cultures and religions for many hundreds of years for religious practices, for announcing important information and also for space clearing. When you clear a space with bells the room feels clean, uplifted and fresh. There are many different types of bells that you can use.

There are small and large Balinese bells, the small bells are used for smaller spaces and you can use the large bells for larger homes and spaces, Tibetan bells, Nepalese bells and many more.

It is important that you choose a bell that feels right for you, you need to take note how it feels in your hand, is it too heavy or too light? Do you like the sound of the bell? Each bell has its own unique sound. Try many different kinds of bells out and see if you prefer a higher toned bell or a bell with a lower tone. Some people even like to look further into the bell to see how it was made, where it was made and who made it.

The reason it is so important to have a bell that sounds right for you is because if you have bell that doesn't sound right to you or is out of tune it will be counterproductive for you when you are space clearing. The sound will not clear out the negative energy, it will make you feel frustrated and could increase the negative energy so be very careful about the bell that you select.

How to space clear with bells

Start at the entrance to your office or in the room which you would like to space clear, focus on what your intention is. Walk clockwise around your office or room ringing the bell in each corner of the room.

When you have rung the bell in each corner of the room stand in the center of the room and ring your bell one or two more times. Listen to the sound of the bell, notice how differently it sounds once you have cleared the room. You will know that the room or your office has been successfully space cleared by the sound of the bell because it will resonate a lot more clearly and will have a wonderful uplifting feel to it.

Open your windows up if you can after you have cleared your office so that all of the old energy can leave.

Singing bowls

In the same way that clapping or using bells can clear energy in your office using a singing bowl can also help you to space clear your work place. A singing bowl is a wonderful tool to create positive energy in your work environment, it is great to be used regularly because the more you use it and get used to using it the more powerful the bowl becomes and the better it will sound.

Singing bowls each have their own beautiful tone, it is important that you find the right bowl for you when you are looking to buy one. Just as I have said about purchasing a bell it is the same thing with singing bowls, look for a bowl that is the right size for your hand and has the right sound for you. Make sure you get a chance to try the singing bowl before you buy it. Each bowl needs to be sold with its own pillow to rest on and a wooden mallet.

How to use your Singing Bowl

Take a deep breath in and breathe out, relax and focus on your intention think about what you would like to happen when you use your singing bowl for example you would like to uplift the energy in your work place and clear out any stale energy.

It is important that you wake your singing bowl up by striking it four times with the mallet once in the north, once in the south, once in the east and once in the west. When you are on the last strike you will need to carefully move the mallet around the bowl to create the humming sound. This can take practice so keep trying if it doesn't work the first time. Try to balance the singing bowl on top of your thumb and fingers.

Once you have woken the singing bowl up carry the bowl around in your non-dominant hand on its cushion if you want to, or just resting on your fingertips while you strike the bowl with the mallet and move the mallet around the outside of the singing bowl to create the beautiful sound. Remember to focus on your intention and start walking from your front door clockwise around each room in your work place striking the singing bowl with the mallet and moving the mallet around until the sound finishes. Open the windows up in your office to let any stagnant energy out.

When you are finished walking around your work place stand still and clear your own energy by striking the mallet against your singing bowl, feel the sound vibrate up and down your body.

Drums

The drum is a very powerful space clearing tool, just like bells and singing bowls can uplift and clear energy drums can very quickly clear the energy and heal people in a room or space. The drum will bring balance to a work place, it balances out the feminine and masculine energies.

Each drum has its own unique sound which can change depending on the weather and time of day, this is because drums are made out of animal skin which tightens or loosens according to the moisture in the air.

It is totally up to you what type of drum you would like to use to space clear, I find that it is best if you use a traditional Native American style hand held drum because they create a beautiful sound and have a lot of positive energy attached to them if they are made with love and dedicated correctly.

The drum is a sacred tool to the Native American people so it is important that you treat your drum with respect, it is not a toy.

How to use a drum to space clear

Take a deep breath in, breathe out, hold your drum close to you and focus on your intention on space clearing your work place. When you are ready and you have your intention clear in your mind allow energy to build inside you. Hold your drum by the tying strings at the back of the drum in your non-dominant hand.

You can use your dominant hand or a drum stick to hit the drum. Start drumming with two beats, like the sound of your heartbeat, make sure that your wrist is relaxed when you hit the drum. Relax and find the energy inside you, find the rhythm that you need. The drumming sound is so powerful it will clear your energy as well as your work place's energy.

Drum in the corner of each room. Remember to focus on your intention and start walking from your front door clockwise around each room in your work place drumming with your hand or drum stick. Keep drumming until you feel that the energy is clear, when you are finished hold the drum to your heart and feel yourself relax and become uplifted. Open the windows up in your work place to let any stagnant energy out.

DE-CLUTTERING/CLEANING YOUR WORK PLACE

You have just read about some of the different tools available to help you to space clear your office or work place but there is also another easy space clearing technique that you can do it is to de-clutter and clean your work place. When you clean and clear the clutter from your work place you are allowing the positive energy to flow through your office or work place, you will feel the energy change instantly within your business and your office.

If you have too much clutter or too many items or objects in your work place there will be pockets of stagnant energy. Stagnant energy clings to items that you do not use very often so it is important that you take note of what you do use regularly or what you can get rid of or pack away.

How to de-clutter your work place

The first step to de-cluttering and cleaning your work place is to go through your items in your office or work place. If you have any old items that are broken, cracked or not working it may be time for you to get rid of or fix these items. Remember when you get rid of old broken items you are making room for positive new energy to enter your business and work place.

The second step is to sort through your items in your office or work place room by room when you can. This can be a big job so try to set aside time when you can, you do not have to de-clutter the whole house in one day. Focus on one room at a time so that you don't get overwhelmed. Have a pile of things that you definitely want to keep, a pile that you want to donate or give away to friends/family, a maybe pile and a throw out junk pile.

After you have put all of your items into piles it is important that you throw your junk items immediately, take your donation items and put them in your car if you have one or near the front door so that you remember to give them away. It is also important that you go through the maybe pile and be very clear about whether you need to or want to keep the item, if you don't need it or really want it throw it out or donate it to someone else. When you are ready put all of the things that you want to keep away in their own special places so that you can have your office clutter free where the positive energy can flow freely.

It is also important that you regularly clean your work place to get rid of any dust, dirt or energy that has built up. By cleaning the floors, benches, windows and any other surfaces around your office and work place you are actively space clearing your environment. This sounds like a normal thing for people to do but some people have become so busy in their everyday lives that they have forgotten the importance of doing simple things like cleaning and de-cluttering.

When you have finished cleaning your work place you may like to use one of the space clearing methods in this book to finish clearing the energy around your office as well.

MUSIC

Music is great for the soul and great to lift energy up in your work place. When you play high vibrational music or music that makes you feel good it really can make a huge difference to how you feel and how your work place feels as well. Nature based sounds such as birds singing, running water, the ocean, the sound of rain or relaxation music such as the Native American flute and drums, instrumental music or even Tibetan monks chanting are all very popular types of music that can be played to uplift and clear the energy in your work place.

Some people choose to play very loud powerful music such as opera or rock music to blast out the negative energy from their business and work place. You may choose to play your favorite music on CDs or on your iPod.

It doesn't really matter which type of music or what sound you use, the most important thing is that you feel positive, empowered and can clearly state your intention of clearing your work space while you have the music playing.

Remember as I have said earlier it is important to be mindful of your co-workers and customers when you are playing music so try to take that into account when you are selecting the music or play your own music after hours when everyone else has left the work place.

CLEARING THE ENERGY WITH POSITIVE THOUGHTS AND INTENTIONS

To space clear your office or work place you can use some of the tools and techniques that I have written about in the previous pages such as using the incense or sage to smudge your office, but if any of these tools or techniques do not suit you there is another way to space clear without using anything other than your own mind and positive intentions.

Some people who may be living away from their main work place or who are not able to physically get to space clear their office can do so from a distance by using their own mind to clear the energy in their office.

It is very easy to clear the energy in your office from a distance, all you need to do is focus on and see each room in your office. Imagine yourself walking through your office, go into each room and see yourself standing in the middle of each room in your office.

When you can see yourself in each room imagine white light circling around the room going into all of the corners of the room. As you imagine white light circling and clearing the energy in each room ask in your mind for all negativity to be removed from that room. Visualize all of the white light moving out of the room through the doorways and out through the windows. You should then imagine that your whole office is now shining brightly with clean and clear bright white energy.

The Mountain Resort and the Spirit

I have had many experiences with space clearing homes, offices and even pieces of land but one of the most unexpected space clearing experiences occurred when I was running one of my spiritual retreats in a mountain resort. I used this resort a couple of times a year to run my weekend retreats, and on one occasion I showed up to set up the normal smaller function room that I used to teach in. When I checked in to the resort I was told by the staff member that the function room had been converted to a restaurant, so I was shown to a bigger brighter room further away from reception.

On the first day of the retreat I spoke to a staff member from the resort, he asked me what kind of function I was running and I explained to him that it was a spiritual retreat about psychic development. When he found out what I was teaching he asked if he could speak to me away from my group. I was unsure what he would say but I agreed to talk to him away from the group.

When we went away from the group the staff member told me that he and some of the other staff members thought that there was a ghost in the resort, specifically in the old function room that is now the restaurant, they all felt scared in this room and this was the room where I was supposed to be teaching my retreat for the weekend.

This is was a great experience to be able to teach my students so I went to investigate with the staff member. As I walked into the dark room I could feel a strong male presence there, this was not a friendly energy, he felt very angry and he had an old feeling about him. He was not happy about being disturbed and was not happy about all of these people changing the room around.

I left the room with the staff member and asked him what he and the other staff had experienced or felt in the room, I did not tell him what I initially felt or saw. He said that many of the staff were scared in that room because they felt like someone was watching them particularly when they were in the room by themselves.

A female staff member had set the function room up with tea light candles on each table, after the function was over she went into the room to tidy up, she blew out all of the candles and went into the kitchen. When she returned a minute later the room was lit up again with every candle lit on the tables, no one else was working in that area or would have had time to light all of the candles in such a short amount of time. The male staff member said this female was so freaked out she didn't want to work in that room anymore. He also said other staff members had experienced many different things including books jumping off the bookshelf at them in that room, near the old stone fireplace.

I asked the staff member if he wanted me to try and help clear this space. I said to him that I would need to have permission from the owner of the resort to do this. He checked with the owner and they were very open to me trying to help space clear the room as long as it was kept quiet and did not interfere with any of the staff or guests.

The retreat went on as usual I taught the students about psychic protection and space clearing as well as many other things but on the last day I asked the students if they would like to go into a room to feel its energy. They all agreed. I didn't tell them anything about the room or what had happened there I wanted to see if they would be able to pick up on the old man's energy.

As soon as we entered the room a few of the students could feel a presence and some said they felt it was angry. A couple *of them even pointed to the fireplace. After they shared what they felt in the room I let them know what I had felt and what had been going on in the room. I told them that I would be space clearing this room and if they wanted to stay they could stay and help or if they wanted to leave that was OK as well. They all wanted to stay and help.*

This was not something I had planned prior to arriving at the resort but it ended up being a great experience for the students to feel spirits and learn how to move negative spirits or energy on.

To clear the old man's spirit out of the room I began by spraying my protection spray, which is a spritzer of essential oils, into each corner of the room. As I sprayed I asked for all negativity to be removed and I asked for protection for myself and everyone in the room.

After clearing the room with spray, I then asked for all of the students to hold hands with me included in a circle. I lit three candles and put them in the center of the circle and I asked all of the students to hold hands and to focus on the candles and ask for the spirit to be sent to the light. I called upon Archangel Michael and asked him to come and take this lost spirit to the light. I felt the old man resisting but I continued to ask three times, on the third time I felt a heat come over me and I felt that the male spirit had left.

As soon as the spirit left the room the energy was a lot calmer and cooler. The students felt the change immediately. I explained to them that it was important that we snuff the three candles out we were not to blow the candles out to make sure that the energy had been released.

Please note that sending this spirit to the light does not harm it, in any way it actually helps him to grow spiritually and not be stuck in that room. The male spirit was getting frustrated being there because he didn't understand why so many strangers were in his room and moving things around.

This resort that I was teaching my retreat out of was built on a massive piece of traditional farming land on top of a mountain. The resort's main office and function room was the original cottage that had been renovated and converted. This male spirit may have been an original owner of the land or a drover or cattleman that had once lived there.

The owner of the resort and staff members are now much happier working in the converted function room which is now a busy restaurant and I feel that the old male spirit is much happier as well being reconnected with his family in spirit.

CHAPTER FOUR

HOW TO KEEP THE ENERGY POSITIVE IN A WORK PLACE

It is not only important to space clear your office or work place it is also important that once you have lifted the energy in your work place you maintain the new energy and that you keep your work place and everyone in it feeling positive. You can do this in a variety of ways through fresh air, sunlight, green plants, or by using the principles of Feng Shui, crystals, aromatherapy and much more. I have discussed a few of these topics earlier in this book and explained how to use them to space clear your work place, I will now explain to you how to use some of these tools and techniques to keep the energy in your work place free flowing, positive and uplifting.

Feng Shui

What is Feng Shui?

Feng Shui is an ancient Chinese art form which was developed over 3,000 years ago to create harmony between people and their environment and to enhance people's health and wellbeing, this is achieved by arranging the energy in and around the environment.

Feng Shui is used to create positive energy in all areas of the home and office, it involves gathering the good energy or 'chi' so that you can reduce the negative energy. Feng Shui shows that every living and non-living thing has its own energy. We are constantly coming into contact with all of these different energies everywhere that we go, so it is important that we create a safe, positive space for ourselves in our home and office.

If you follow the principles of Feng Shui you will be able to balance the energy in each room of your office this will then help to promote good health and abundance for everyone who works there. When you change the furniture placement and the surroundings in your office you lift the energy up which allows you to change your life for the better. In Feng Shui you need to look at your office as a whole system because each room and each part of the office is connected energetically to the other.

You do not need to be a Feng Shui expert to start applying Feng Shui principles to your office. There are a lot of easy Feng Shui hints and tips that you can easily apply to your office straight away.

When you start to think about how to use Feng Shui to create positive energy in your office it can be helpful to identify which part of your office you think may need the most help or needs more positive energy. For example, you may already feel great about your staffroom and boardroom room, but your reception area or personal office may be in need of some extra positive energy or decluttering.

Look at how the Feng Shui energy runs throughout your whole office. Do all of the rooms in your office have positive energy or the ability to maintain positive energy? Does the energy flow freely or does it get stuck before it reaches certain areas or rooms in your office? Make sure that you check even small spaces such as cupboards, sheds, attics and the office kitchen to see how the energy feels in there. If an office has positive energy flowing through and around it, anyone that works in or visits the office will feel uplifted and have a greater sense of well-being.

Once you have identified the rooms or areas that you would like to add positive energy to, you can start to make a list of where you would like to start implementing the Feng Shui principles. Remember as I have said earlier in this book with space clearing it is all about the intent that you put out to the Universe, you need to put an intent out that you want your office to feel positive, uplifted and abundant for all who live and visit there.

It doesn't matter if you work from home in a home office or studio, or if you work in an office which is located outside of the home, it is very important that you pay attention to the energy that you have in and around your office.

If you can pay attention to clearing out any old or stagnant energy you will notice a big difference in the energy of all of the people that work in the office. The customers and clients will also feel the energy when they enter the business or office as well.

When you space clear an office you are making room for positive new energy to be attracted in to the business. When new energy is attracted in your business's productivity will increase, the staff will be happier and healthier and the finances will increase.

Workers all around the world spend many hours per day or night at their work places, so it is very important that they are surrounded by as much positive energy as they can be otherwise it can affect their health. If a person doesn't feel right in their work place it can affect their health, their work productivity and their relationships with their co-workers, bosses, clients and customers.

Even if you can't change much around your office you can put things into place in your own personal work area or desk, that will help you to space clear your cubicle, desk or personal workspace. Just as you can apply the principles of Feng Shui to a whole office you can also apply this on a smaller personal scale, you can apply Feng Shui to your desk.

Here is some essential Feng Shui information that relates to all of the different parts of your office. This information can help you to keep the energy positive in your office:

The front door
It is very important that you have a very strong, visually attractive front door so that you can welcome good energy into your office.

Your office will gain energy and nourishment from your front door, this is why the front door is called the 'Mouth of Chi'.

Your front door needs to be able to attract and help the flow of good Feng Shui energy into your business and office instead of making the energy weak or negative, or even pushing it away.

The lounge room/staff room

It is very important that you have good Feng Shui in your lounge/staff room because this is where you and your staff members and visitors may spend a lot of time. Your lounge/staff room should have good lighting, clean and clear air, have everything organized in its own place and be uncluttered.

To check the flow of energy in your lounge/staff room stand at the entrance to the room and see how the energy feels. Can you imagine seeing where the energy flows to? If you can, see if you can see anything that blocks the good Feng Shui. Is an obstacle in the room that may slow the energy down or block the energy from flowing freely, for example if water was to flow through your lounge room where would the water flow to?

When you arrange the furniture in your lounge/staff room try to create a room that feels right for you and the other staff members and guests, you may aim for a room that makes everyone have a feeling of being positively connected, social and comfortable.

The kitchen

In addition to the staff room your office kitchen may be another part of your office where you spend a lot of time with your staff members and clients socializing, it is also a very important part of your office because this is where you store your food and gain your nourishment from. The kitchen was considered to be the heart of the home (or in this case, the heart of your office) since ancient times; use Feng Shui to make it a happy and healthy.

To maintain positive energy it is essential that you have good nutrition because good nutrition makes good energy which then makes good Feng Shui energy for your work place, business and the people who work in it.

It is not only nutrition that we should focus on when looking at the energy of your kitchen it is also important to look at how your kitchen feels. Is the kitchen well balanced and clutter free? Does the energy feel happy and positive in your kitchen?

There are various things that you should pay attention to when you are looking at the Feng Shui energy in your kitchen they are as follows:

Δ *Keep your kitchen clutter free*

Δ *Try not to have too many items on your bench tops, this includes kitchen utensils, bowls and electrical items*

Δ *Have fresh air in your kitchen with windows open to let natural sunlight in*

Δ *Have a green plant, fresh green herbs, flowers and a bowl of fruit in your kitchen*

The bathroom and toilet

Some people may not realize the importance of the bathroom and toilet areas in relation to their design, Feng Shui energy and location. Bathrooms and toilets are just as important as the kitchen, office and boardrooms. In fact it is especially important that you do pay attention to these areas because they are associated with the water element and they do tend to leak energy. If you have a bathroom or toilet that is well maintained and has good Feng Shui energy you are creating a positive, calm and healing energy for your office.

One of the most important things for you to check for both the bathroom and the toilet is to make sure that there are no dripping taps and that all of the plumbing fixtures are clean and working well. If you have a dripping tap in Feng Shui it is believed to encourage you to waste money or the money is flushed down the drain.

There are various things that you should pay attention to when you are looking at the Feng Shui energy in your bathroom and toilet they are as follows:

Δ *It is important to make sure that you can keep warm in the bathroom in winter months, have heat lamps or try to make the space warm for the cooler months.*

Δ *Try to have things that are visually pleasing to you and other people in your office, such as pictures or designs that you will all like.*

Δ *The lighting is important in the bathroom particularly for women who need to do their makeup, so make sure you have adequate lighting.*

Δ *Mirrors are important in the bathroom not only so you can see yourself but also to bring in good Feng Shui energy through the water element.*

FENG SHUI YOUR DESK

Even if you can't change much around your office you can put things into place in your own personal work area or desk that will help you to space clear your cubicle, desk or personal work space. Just as you can apply the principles of Feng Shui to a whole office you can also apply this on a smaller personal scale to your desk. Look at the Feng Shui Bagua map and relate the colors and the different areas to your desk. For example if you want to focus on your wealth and prosperity, focus on the back left hand corner of your desk, consider putting a jade plant or citrine crystal in this part of your desk.

The placement of your desk is one of the most important Feng Shui adjustments you can make. Desk placement is very important for Feng Shui, if possible try to put your desk facing the front door of your office in the power position. The power position is important because it means that you can see as much of the room as possible and also the front door when you are sitting at your desk.

The diagram below shows you the best place to put your desk in your office, if possible.

Not everyone has the opportunity to have their own office space where they can choose where to put their desk. If you work in an office with multiple desks or desks that face each other try to do your best to create your own personal space. If possible try not to sit face to face or back to back with your co-workers, try to sit side by side or stagger the desks for privacy. It is also very important to try and create your own

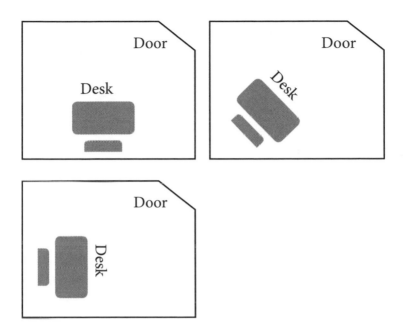

personal work space, you can do this by placing happy photos on your desk, a good Feng Shui plant such as jade, crystals and anything else that makes you feel happy while you are at your desk.

Another important thing is that you need to make sure that you keep your desk uncluttered. A cluttered office or desk means that you have a cluttered mind, an organized desk attracts creative and positive energy in. Organize your desk in a way that best suits you and your work place, try to keep at least half of the desk clutter free at all times.

CRYSTALS

At the beginning of chapter three in this book I have written about the healing power of crystals and how to use crystal gridding to space clear and protect your office. There are many different types of crystals in the world and each has their own special healing powers. I would like to show you some additional crystals that you can use to enhance the energy in your office to keep everyone in the office feeling healthy and positive.

It is important that you learn what each crystal does so that you can use the right crystal to achieve the intention that you have, for example you can use rose quartz for love and relationships. You may like to wear the crystals in a pendant, as a bracelet, on a ring or have them in and around your office, on display in bowls, in a crystal grid pattern on a table or hang them as a sun catcher near your windows.

Here is a list of some of the more common crystals that you can use in and around your office. I have focused on categorizing the crystals into groups. Each group relates to an emotional feeling or energy or what you want to achieve by using that crystal.

Balance

Life is very hectic, for most people it can be extremely hard to find balance between your work, family, friendships and relationship. Do you feel like you need to have better balance in your life? Or do you feel that your work and family life is balanced but you just need to find more time to balance your own mind, body and spirit?

It is hard to find balance in our lives when we are busy racing around during the day, that is why it is so important to create a positive environment at home, so you can recharge and rebalance yourself.

The following crystals can help you to uplift your energy to find balance again in your life:

Chrysocolla

Chrysocolla enhances positive energy and gets rid of any negative energy in and around a person. Chrysocolla helps to balance out a person's mind, body and spiritual energy.

To find your own sense of balance and to enhance your inner confidence and personal power, wear Chrysocolla or place it in and around your office.

Turquoise

Turquoise is a wonderful balancer and healer, it helps people to balance out their energy and gives people a strong sense of peace and serenity. If you wear or hold a piece of Turquoise you can uplift your energy, relieve your stress and bring positive energy into your life. You can also place turquoise in and around your office wherever you feel you would most benefit from it.

Watermelon Tourmaline

Watermelon Tourmaline is a very powerful healing crystal which helps to balance out the male and female energies within a person. It can also remove any stagnant, confused or angry energy to create a positive harmonious energy in an environment.

Watermelon Tourmaline encourages people to have a calm, balanced energy and state of mind. You may like to wear a Watermelon Tourmaline piece of jewelry, pendant or necklace or place it in and around your office.

Change

Changes in your life are unavoidable; you may be on the verge of some big changes such as changing jobs, having a baby, staff leaving, starting to study, changing your business or moving offices. Whatever the change is that is happening around you it is very important not to fear change, try to have a positive mindset and welcome in the new energy that comes with the changes in your life.

The following crystals can be very helpful in times of change:

Blue Aventurine

Blue Aventurine is great to use in times of change because it is a powerful crystal that helps to increase your energy and give you a positive outlook on life. Blue Aventurine also has a calming effect on people's emotions, this would be very helpful for anyone who is going through the process of change in their lives.

Fuchsite

Fuchsite is a wonderful crystal which helps people to solve their problems, it also helps people to relieve emotional shock and enables people to feel positive and inspired. This is a very good crystal to have with you during times of change.

Communication

Communication is the key to any successful relationship that is why it is so important that we communicate correctly with our loved ones, friends, work colleagues and any other people that we come in contact with.

People can communicate in various different ways such as verbally, non-verbally, with sign language and by writing. It doesn't matter which form of communication that you use however it is important that you communicate in a clear, concise and positive way so that other people can understand what it is that you want to convey to them.

If everyone in your work place is communicating effectively with each other it will help to keep the energy positive in your work place because there will be less conflicts or misunderstandings and more peace and happiness.

You can improve your communication and the communication of everyone else in your work place by using some of the following crystals:

Blue Lace Agate

Blue lace agate is a calming, uplifting crystal, it encourages peaceful communication. Blue lace agate also helps to reduce disagreements by helping people to communicate with each other and by calming the energy around the office.

Larimar

Larimar is a very soothing crystal which is great for helping people to express their emotions. Larimar releases any emotional blocks or attachments and allows people to open up to love and nurturing. This crystal is very good for helping people to communicate openly in a loving way that benefits everyone.

Energy

Many of us want or need more energy to do the things that we need to or want to do during our busy days. There are some crystals which can help you to feel reenergised and that can also help lift the energy in and around your office. These crystals can help you to feel more energetic, passionate, active and motivated.

The following crystals can help to bring you positive energy, passion and motivation:

Yellow Apatite

Yellow Apatite is a great crystal that gets rid of many toxins in your body it also helps to get rid of any stagnant energy in and around your office. Yellow Apatite also helps people to feel reenergised, passionate and motivated.

Tangerine Quartz

Tangerine Quartz helps to energize you, it gives you motivation to move forward and an extra energy lift. Tangerine quartz can also help with building and maintaining a sense of confidence which can then help to keep your energy high and help you to keep motivated. When your energy is positive and you feel motivated and this energy then radiates out of you to everyone else in your work place.

Happiness

Happiness is essential to a healthy life, if you can lead a happy and balanced life you and your loved ones will benefit from it. Everyone is an individual, each person has their own likes and dislikes and things that make them happy. What makes one person happy may not make another person happy, we are all different.

It is really important that you find out what makes you happy so that you can continue to have positive energy around you. There are many different crystals that can help enhance the happiness in your life, they are as follows:

Citrine

Citrine brings positive energy, happiness and enthusiasm to anyone that is wearing it or to the space that it is placed in. It is also an abundance crystal so it brings in new finances, abundance in happiness and love and abundance in all good things in your life.

Citrine also helps to motivate people by opening up people's creativity and by helping them to express themselves so that they can feel happy and at peace with their lives.

Peridot

Peridot is a very powerful crystal which cleanses your energy, reduces stress and opens your heart to happiness and new beginnings. Peridot also enhances your self-confidence and helps you to move forward and take responsibility for your life in a positive way.

Remember that crystals can help to heal you but it is still important that you stick to your regular medications and/or natural therapies which are recommended to you by qualified medical practitioners.

MALA BEADS

What are mala beads?

A mala is a strand of beads, traditionally used in Buddhist religious practices such as during meditation. A mala is usually made up of 108 beads that are all strung together by strong string or elastic to create a necklace or bracelet. The mala beads are used in a similar way to the Roman Catholic 'Rosary' beads they are used as focus point during prayers and meditation and they are also used for counting during mantra meditations.

Malas are always made with round, small beads that are usually 7–10mm in size. The mala beads are traditionally made with many different things such as bodhi seeds, wood, crystal gemstones, yak bones and lotus seed beads. Each bead is shaped and made smooth to allow the user to easily move their fingers over the bead.

Many people who practice yoga and meditate use mala beads. If you don't practice yoga or meditate mala beads can still be a very powerful focus point for you to put your positive intentions to. You may like to wear a mala necklace or bracelet or have it in your drawer or on your desk at work, this can help you to maintain the positive energy in your work place.

HOW TO USE MALA BEADS

If you are interested in learning how to use mala beads it is quite simple. The first thing that you need to do after getting your own set of mala beads is to focus upon finding the largest mala bead on your bracelet or necklace, this large bead is called the guru of the mala and it is usually found in the middle of the bottom of string of mala beads where the string is knotted together or tied together.

Once you have found the guru mala bead, put the mala bead that is on the right of your guru mala bead in between your middle finger and thumb. Take time now on this first mala bead to focus on your breathing, breathe in and breathe out. The next thing to focus on is what you are trying to achieve, what is your intent. For example you may like to focus on having a positive and abundant energy in your office.

When you are ready you pass your fingers over each mala bead and focus your intention with each bead as it passes through your fingers. Remember that there are usually 108 mala beads on a string so you would be putting your intention into 108 beads and thinking positive thoughts each time (there are also mala beads that come in smaller numbers but the main one I am focusing on is the 108 mala). If you can do this on a regular basis think how positive the energy will be around you and your office.

If you wish to keep the positive energy and intentions with you throughout the day you may choose to wear your mala beads as a necklace, bracelet or put them in a special pouch that is protected in your wallet or bag.

If you choose not to wear your mala beads when you are not using them that is OK, you may like to put the mala beads in a special place that is safe in your desk or you can put them on display on your desk.

The most important thing to do with your mala beads is that you treat the mala beads with respect and you keep your positive intentions going when you are holding them.

MEDITATION

Meditation is a great stress reducer and a great way to relax and quiet your mind, it not only helps you to feel more positive about life it can even help you psychologically and physically. There are many other benefits that meditation can do for you, it can help you to remain calm and positive, it can help you to focus better on your work and/or studies and it can even help you to relax your mind for a better sleep.

To some people who have never had a chance to meditate before it can seem a bit daunting but I can assure you that there are many different forms of mediation and it is actually quite simple to meditate. You do not need to be a Buddhist Monk or a Yoga master to be able to meditate all you need is approximately ten minutes in a quiet space by yourself to start off with, it does not have to be complicated.

There is no set time that you must stick to if you want to meditate, you can meditate at any time of the day that suits you. You may like to meditate as soon as you wake up in the morning to start your day, or at lunch time in the middle of the day to give you positive energy to continue your day, or even at the end of the day to help you relax before you go to sleep.

There are many different meditation techniques but I will just give you a few examples here, it is totally up to you what type of meditation technique you would like to use. You may like to try a few different techniques to see what suits you best. Remember that it is not hard, the whole purpose of meditation is to calm your thoughts so that you can have positive energy and inner balance.

How to meditate quickly and easily

There are a few easy steps that you can take to start meditating they are as follows:

1. *Take some time out of your day, try to set aside approximately ten minutes when you won't be disturbed by anyone.*
2. *Go to a quiet place where you know that you won't be disturbed while you meditate, it may be an office room or even outside in a park or garden.*
3. *Sit or lie comfortably.*
4. *Focus on your breathing, breathe in and out in long deep breaths. Focus on relaxing all the muscles in your body.*
5. *Calm your mind and let go of anything that is stressing you or making you upset. Be present only in the moment, try not to think about all of the chores or work that you need to do that day.*
6. *See yourself shining brightly full of white light from the tips of your toes all the way to the top of your head. Imagine that you are a clear vessel with white*

light pouring out of every part of your body. After you see yourself shining brightly, imagine that you are surrounded by a big bubble of gold light. This gold light will protect your energy and allow you to remain positive.

7. *After you have surrounded yourself in gold light, focus on your breathing again, think about all of the things that you are thankful for in your life. Smile and bring your awareness back to your physical body and the area that you are meditating in.*

8. *When you are feeling happy and relaxed, stretch your arms up above your head, shake your hands and feet to get the energy flowing and enjoy the positive relaxed energy that is flowing throughout your whole body.*

If you can try to practice meditating on a regular basis you will notice how much meditation will improve your life.

Gratitude and Positive Attitude

You may be wondering why I would be writing about gratitude in a book about clearing the energy in your office and work place. The answer to that is simple, your own personal energy affects everyone and everything in your work place. If you are upbeat, positive and grateful everybody in the work place benefits from it.

It is important that you try and practice gratitude every day. It doesn't matter what religion or belief system you have, if you don't take time to be grateful you will never have more happiness in your life. If you are grateful you will be given more happiness and you will have more abundance in your life.

Gratitude and a positive attitude to life can change all of the areas in your life from your financial situation, your health, your career and your relationships.

Are you grateful?

How do you feel about the following areas: your family, career, relationships, health and finances?

Is there an area where you feel you could add more positive energy to it?

Is there an area where you feel it is already going really well for you and you may already feel that it is a positive area that you are grateful for? Have you considered that may be this area is going so well for you because you are already grateful for that area? An example of this may be in your relationship area, you may be thankful and grateful for your partner every day and as a result of this positive energy and gratitude you will receive even more positive energy in your relationship area.

When you are feeling grateful and have a positive attitude for the people and things in your life you will attract in more of these people and things to be grateful for. It is important that you try not to focus in on the negative things that are occurring in your life, because energy flows where your attention goes. If you are thinking of negative things you may manifest and make negative things happen.

There are so many little things and big things to be grateful for every day. I am always grateful for the roof over my head for myself and my family and for the food that we have to eat that sustains and nourishes us.

What are you grateful for? It can be an uplifting and positive experience to write down a list of thing that you are grateful for. Here are some examples of things that you may like to write down:

△ *I am grateful for my job because it gives me the finances to provide for myself and my family.*

△ *I love my friends and family and I am grateful for having them in my life.*

△ *I have so much energy and I am grateful that I can enjoy running, walking and exercising to keep my body fit and healthy.*

△ *Today is a great day and I am grateful because we are all happy and healthy.*

Gratitude and your relationships
Gratitude and a positive attitude make relationships flourish. If your relationship area is shining brightly you yourself will be full of positive energy and this positive energy will radiate out of you to every person that you come in contact with.

Gratitude and your health
Your relationship area is not the only area that you should focus your gratitude and positive attitude on. Your health and your family's health is the other area that is extremely important.

Try to be thankful and grateful for every part of your body and for your health. When you are grateful for your body you will notice a change in your energy and the way that you see yourself, you may not be so quick to judge what you look like or be so hard on yourself about your physical appearance.

When you feel grateful you will begin to feel more positive about your life, this in turn will influence how other people relate to you and/or how you relate to them.

Gratitude for your finances and work

Another area that would benefit from you having a positive attitude and gratitude is your financial and work area. This can be a difficult thing to do if you don't currently have a job, are in financial difficulty or you are currently in a job that you are unhappy in.

In these cases the most important thing to do is to start thinking about something positive that you can be grateful for. For example you may be grateful that you have enough money today to pay your rent or your mortgage and to have enough food on the table in your home to eat.

Remember you want to focus on the positive things in your life that you can be grateful for not the negative things or things that you don't yet have.

If you can have a positive attitude and be grateful in some of or all of these areas in your life you will be well on your way to creating a much more positive energy for yourself, everyone in your home, office and your life.

SUNLIGHT/NATURAL LIGHTING

Have you ever noticed that you feel drained after being at work or other places where you are constantly stuck under fluorescent lighting? Do you sometimes go hours without being able to see the sky or feel the sun on your face? If you have answered yes to both or one of these questions you are not alone, this is becoming quite a common thing for people who are leading very busy lives.

Some people are becoming so disconnected from the natural world including the sun and sky, they are forgetting the importance of natural sunlight. The sun re-energizes us, warms us and brightens up our energy it also provides us with natural lighting and provides the essential vitamin D. Vitamin D is essential for our bodies because it helps your body absorb calcium and phosphorus which are two very important minerals for bone and tooth growth.

There are many people who are deficient in vitamin D because they do not have access to natural sunlight, this can sometimes be due to where they live such as people who live in very cold climates in the Northern Hemisphere. Other people who may be deficient in vitamin D are the elderly, sick, people who wear full head and body coverings, people who have very dark skin.

If someone is deficient in vitamin D this can lead to S.A.D, Seasonal Affective Disorder, this is quite common in people who don't get enough sunlight in the winter months and it can lead to depression.

If you live in an areas where you do get enough sunlight, make the most of it. Too much sun is not a good idea though because of skin cancer, sunburn etc. but a bit of sunlight is required each day for us to remain healthy.

Try to open your blinds, curtains and windows to let the

sunshine come into your work space or office. By letting the sunshine in you are recharging the energy in your work space and you are adding positive energy to it as well. If you can't access windows easily, try to get outside and put your face up to the sun for a few minutes each day, you will instantly feel your energy lift.

HIMALAYAN ROCK SALT LAMPS

Himalayan rock salt lamps not only look beautiful they are wonderful to help attract and keep positive energy in the work place. The Himalayan rock salt lamps also have amazing healing properties. The healing energy from these lamps are claimed to help with mental health disorders, colds, headaches and respiratory problems. These lamps are natural, they are made up from salt that came from oceans which are millions of years old. This Himalayan salt is pure and it is found in salt beds that are deep inside the Himalayan Mountains.

The Himalayan rock salt lamps are nature's best ioniser, this is because the way that the lamp works is similar to an ioniser. The salt lamp needs to be heated for its healing properties to work. When the lamp is turned on and heats up it attracts water molecules from the air which then binds the negative ions with the excess positive ions. Some examples of positive ions are electrical smog, cigarette smoke, pollution, bacteria and dust. Negative ions are purely natural ions that can be found in nature. You can find pure negative ions in the air after storms, if you are near the ocean, near waterfalls and various other natural places.

When the negative ion connects with the positive ion it gets rid of the positive ion therefore it cleans and clears the air. The Himalayan salt lamps can also help to reduce radiation so it is a good idea to put a salt lamp near your electrical devices. Electrical devices are all around us at work and at home. Most people have televisions, computers, laptops, air conditioners or fans, telephones or mobile phones and iPod or CD players. Each of these electrical items create positive ions which is electric smog.

Electric smog is when the energy and air deteriorates, this can lead to many health problems. Many people may not even be aware of how much electrical smog is around them and their work place. Think about your office or work place— do you have a television set, laptop, iPod, CD player, air conditioner or mobile phone running while you are in there? Electric smog can definitely affect you in a negative way, mentally and physically.

The Himalayan salt lamp can help to clear the electric smog by increasing the number of negative ions in a particular area in your office or work place. You can also open the windows regularly in your work place to let the fresh air and sunlight in.

You can put a Himalayan salt lamp anywhere in your work place that suits you and your co-workers but here are some of the best locations to put your salt lamp in your office to lift the energy up and to clear the air:

Δ *In the office near any electrical devices such as computers, laptops and air conditioners. Be aware though that the salt lamp attracts moisture so they do leak a bit of water when they are not turned on, so please do not put them on top of any electrical appliances or surfaces that are not waterproof.*

Δ *In the reception area so that it creates a nice soft pink glow and it also lets people feel relaxed if they are waiting.*

FRESH AIR

You have just read about electric smog and positive ions in the air and as simple as it sounds many people underestimate the importance of fresh air in and around your work place. It is extremely important that you have good quality, clean air for you to breathe. If there is dust or dirt lying in and around the work place this can not only cause health problems such as asthma it can also create stagnant energy in the business.

Good ventilation in the work place is just as important as having a good source of natural sunlight. If possible and if the air quality outside is good and the weather is permitting you should try to open your windows regularly to let fresh air into your work place.

Many people use air conditioners and heaters which recycle the old air in and around the office or work place, this is not good to do all the time. If you do use an air conditioner or heater regularly remember to keep the filters clean and regularly check that the air conditioner and heater are safe and providing clean air for you and everyone in your work place.

If you need to you can use air vents and fans to try and move the stagnant air around in your office or work place. Plants are also good for cleaning the air in your office. Stagnant air is not good for your health and it is not good for the energy in your office.

Flowing fresh air is the best air to have circulating around your work place, it helps to keep the energy positive in your work place and business.

ESSENTIAL OILS

Essential oils are not only used to space clear an office or work place as I have written about earlier, they are also used to lift the energy in a work place to help attract and maintain positive energy. Many essential oils can have a very positive affect on how we feel, by sensing and smelling the different oils you can uplift your own energy and the energy of everyone else in your work place.

Each person has different likes and dislikes, what you may find pleasing to your senses may not appeal to someone else. It is important that you choose your essential oils wisely, ask the other people that work in your work place if they like the smell of the oils that you have chosen before you burn them. Because if you burn oils that have a smell that the other people don't like it will cause negative energy not positive energy.

There are many different types of essential oils that you can buy, make sure that you buy a good quality pure essential oil. Here is a list of the more popular essential oils which you can use to help lift the energy up in your work place:

Δ *Apple*

Δ *Bergamot*

△ *Cedarwood*

△ *Cyprus*

△ *Frankincense*

△ *Geranium*

△ *Jasmine*

△ *Lavender*

△ *Lemon / Citrus*

△ *Neroli*

△ *Peppermint*

△ *Rose*

△ *Sage*

△ *Ylang Ylang*

Before you use any of these oils make sure that you learn or find out about the oils that you intend to use. Read any warnings or contraindications associated with that particular oil before you use it particularly if you or someone in your work place is pregnant or has a specific allergy.

FOOD

Good food and water is essential not only to keep our body alive and strong it is also very important for us socially so we can bond with other people. Food has its own energy, what you eat can definitely affect the way you feel.

The quality of the food you eat is also important. When you are trying to keep yourself feeling happy and healthy take time to look at the food and drinks that you put into your body. Everybody has different likes and dislikes so what may be a great meal for one person may not suit another person. Also each person has different dietary requirements, each body can tolerate different things.

It is important that you listen to what it is that your body is trying to tell you, for example how does your body feel after you eat a hot curry dish? Does it feel good or do you feel like it doesn't agree with you?

Just as food is important for you physically it is also important to the energy in the office. If you have old, stale, expired food lying around on your bench tops, in your cupboards or in your fridge this sends out negative energy.

Try to have fresh fruit and food that is still within its expiry date. Any food that is off, old or out of date clear it out of your office as soon as possible so that you can remove any old stagnant energy. When you remove this old food it makes way for you to add new food into your office, it also declutters your cupboards and fridge so you have more space.

It is not only important to pay attention to clearing any old food out of your office it is also important to have gratitude for your food. You can do this by being thankful for your food, by saying a prayer or blessing if that is your belief or just by savoring your food and not being wasteful.

Try to only cook the amount of food that you need if you do have any extra left over food don't waste it, freeze it or eat it the next day. I know this may sound like a contradiction to what I just said about throwing out old food but this food is fresh and still has good energy. This is a simple thing that many people do, but there are some people that are so busy that they forget to do these things. Some people have become used to being in a throwaway society, they throw things out and waste good things without thinking about it.

Colors in Your Work Place

Many people may not be aware that the color scheme and different colored items in your work place do make a difference to how the space feels. Have you ever walked into an office or place that has very dark purple, dark gray or black walls throughout it? If you have how did it feel to you?

Obviously you can only change the colors and decor in your work place if you are the owner or boss, and each person has their own taste when it comes to decorating. Generally speaking if a room or the inside of a office is painted in really heavy dark colors it can make the room feel heavy, smaller and can hold onto negative or stagnant energy. It is OK to have a feature wall in dark colors or to have darker furniture, just try to balance the darker colors out with lighter walls around it.

To attract and keep the energy positive in your work place it is a good idea to use lighter colors or even a shade of white that you may like. As I have said with the dark colors it is just as important to make sure that you don't have too much white in your work place. Too much white can make a work place feel very clinical, like a hospital. It can also be hard to relax if there aren't any other colors around that your eye can focus on.

If you do have a lot of white in your work place try to make sure that you have different colored artwork, furniture and or soft furnishings such as pillows, rugs, curtains or carpet.

You don't need to just stick to having white colored walls, there are so many beautiful colors out there. Try to see what colors you are intuitively drawn to and see what suits your furniture, business and your work place.

Each color has its own unique energy that it brings into your work place. When selecting the colors for your work place it is a good idea to try and think about what energy you want in that room.

When you are looking at selecting the colors for a particular room remember that everything needs to be done in balance. If you overdo a color you can accidently end up with too much of that energy which then can be counterproductive to what you were originally trying to achieve.

Here is a list of some of the main colors that people may have in their work places and the energy that they can bring into your work place:

Blues

The lighter shades of blue usually are quite relaxing, peaceful and calming. Just remember though that you don't want to overdo it too much with one color. Too much blue especially the darker shades can have the reverse affect energetically, it can make people feel depressed and lethargic.

Reds

There are many different shades of red from maroon right up to tomato red or even some dark pinks and fuchsias. The color red is associated with passion, romance and action. This color is great in small amounts to attract positive energy.

Try not to overdo it with the red colorings because if you have too much red it equals too much passion, which can then attract in anger and or aggression.

Purples

Purple is a mixture of red and blue together it holds great energy for protection, spiritual connection and it is very luxurious. There are many different shades of purple from very light lilac right up to a very dark purple.

Balance is very important so if you are using a dark purple in your office try to stick to using it on a feature wall because too much purple, particularly if it is dark, can have a depressive or stagnant energy.

Greens

Green is such a beautiful healing color, it reminds us of nature and it attracts in healing and abundance energy. All shades of green are very positive, some people prefer a light mint green others may like dark emerald green.

If you don't want to paint your walls green you can add green plants or décor to your office or work place to attract in positive energy. Be aware though because too much green can attract in a lazy, sleepy energy. It is OK if you break the green up in different parts of your work place.

Oranges/brown earth tones

Brown earth tones and shades of orange can bring in a very warm, positive grounded energy into your work place. You do not have to have these colors painted on your walls, you may have polished wooden floors, wooden furniture or have artwork, furnishings or objects which have the earthy brown and orange tones to them.

It is a good idea to have lighter colored walls with heavier earth toned wooden flooring or if you have a lot of wooden furniture. If there is too much wooden furniture, brown earth tones or orange colorings it can make people feel heavy or restless.

Yellows

Yellow is such a bright, happy color it is a wonderful color to attract positive energy into your work place. Yellow is also associated with creativity and inspiration.

Just as the sun brightens up dark spaces, the color yellow can do the same thing. Try to use the yellow color in balance so that you don't cause the energy in the office to become restless.

PAINTING YOUR OFFICE AND MOVING ITEMS AROUND

It is amazing how different the energy in a work place can become when you change the colors of the rooms or change the color of the furniture or soft furnishings. When you paint a room even if you repaint it the same color as it already is you are creating clean, new energy. The room will feel and look clean and the energy will be very high and positive.

If you are renting or leasing a work space you may not be able to change the color of the walls or paint them but you can add posters, paintings, curtains or change the furniture around. Sometimes even the smallest item or piece of color added to a room can lift the energy up enormously.

NATURE/INDOOR PLANTS

Plants are a wonderful addition to your work place, you may like to focus on having indoor plants or have plants outside in your garden. As I have written earlier in the book the healing energy of the color green, indoor plants are a great way to add color and positive energy to your work place.

Plants not only add they also clear the air and create a healthy environment. The ancient art of Feng Shui shows us that there are many plants that you can use inside your work place to balance out and attract positive energy. There are specific plants that are recommended because of the shape and texture of their leaves. Plants which have round, soft leaves attract more positive energy into your work place.

Try to avoid indoor plants that have spiky or pointy leaves because sharp points are not for the energy flow around your work place. Also try to avoid dried flowers or fake plastic flowers, if at all possible it is best use real flowers.

Some of the best indoor plants are:

Aglaonema
The aglaonema plant is a good looking plant that is slow growing and long lasting, they have large, narrow oval leaves on short stems. It's important to keep these plants warm and moist.

Bamboo

The bamboo plant is very good to have in your office, it brings in very good Feng Shui energy. Please see the separate section below on bamboo for more information.

Begonia

The begonia plants are some of the most popular indoor plants, there are many different types of begonia plants. Begonias cannot handle very cold temperatures, too much moisture or strong sunlight.

Croton

The croton plant is made up of a variety of beautiful bright colors such as bright reds, oranges, pinks, purples and yellows. The croton plant prefers warm, humid conditions with lots of water and dappled sunlight.

Ficus

The ficus tree is a very decorative plant that can be potted and kept indoors. The ficus tree needs warmth, humidity and lots of light. These plants do not like to be moved.

Orchids

Orchids are very popular and beautiful plants that have a variety of different shaped and colored flowers. Orchids attract in very good energy into your work place.

Primrose

Potted indoor primroses are a wonderful way to attract in positive energy into your work place. The primrose plant comes in many different beautiful colors and it is made up of many delicate flowers.

African Violets

African violets are very popular indoor plants, these plants come in many different colors and leaf forms. African violets love bright, warm and humid conditions.

LUCKY BAMBOO

Bamboo is a beautiful green plant that is very tough and hard wearing, it is great to have in a small pot indoors because it is very easy to look after and can live for a long time if cared for correctly. In Feng Shui a little bamboo plant is considered to bring good luck.

Bamboo plants

When choosing your bamboo plant there are a few things that you may like to look at to increase the positive energy and good luck in your work place. It is a good idea to try and have the five elements present in your bamboo and bamboo pot. The five elements are fire, water, wood, metal and earth.

You can easily apply all five elements by using the bamboo and pot, for example the bamboo can be planted in a glass or metal pot. If you use a different kind of pot you can add the metal element by tying a coin to it. The earth element is the dirt or rocks which the bamboo is planted in and the water element is taken care of when you water the bamboo. The fire element can be linked in with the metal element if you tie a metal coin to the pot for the metal element you use a red ribbon to tie the coin. The color red is associated with the fire element.

You don't need to go into detail and have all of the five elements for your bamboo plant if you don't want to. I have used just a simple little piece of lucky bamboo plant in a clear glass jar with distilled water in it over the years and it has worked very well.

SCENTED INDOOR PLANTS

There are also some plants that have their own beautiful, unique fragrances which can help to clear the air in and around the work place. Some fragrances and scents can create a balanced and harmonious energy. In Feng Shui certain scents can have a very positive and powerful effect on the energy in your work place.

Here is a list of some of the best scented indoor plants and the energy that each of these plant fragrances can bring in and around your work place:

Miniature Roses—have the highest positive vibration of all plants

Rosemary—is for healing and protection

Lavender—is for relaxation, calming and inner peace

Basil—is for happiness, love and passion

Lemon—is for friendship and purification

Jasmine—is for love and money

Orchids—are for love and friendship

Juniper—is for cleansing

Sage—is for protection
Citrus—is cleansing
Eucalyptus—is for balance and cleansing

FRAGRANT FRESH FLOWERS

You may like to choose to have fresh flowers in your work place to lift the energy up and to add color. Fresh flowers instantly add great energy to your work place. It doesn't matter which flowers you choose it is totally a personal preference in regard to the color, shape, texture and scent of the flowers that you like.

When you do have fresh flowers make sure that you look after them by having them sit in clean water. Once the flowers are dying, limp or dried out it is important that you throw them out and clean out the old stale water so that you don't encourage any stagnant energy.

The Office and the Desks

While writing this chapter I was reminded of a client of mine who is a good example of how important it is to space clear and maintain positive energy in the work place. This client asked me to look at her work place to find out why she was constantly losing staff. She said that staff were very positive and energetic when she first hired them but within a few months they would lose their energy and start to take a lot of sick days or quit their jobs and stop working there.

After hearing this information I told my client that I would need to personally go and see her office so that I could feel what the energy was like there. When I went to my client's office the first thing that I noticed was the arrangement of the desks. There were five desks all together in one room, each of the desks were positioned to face each other.

It is not a good idea to have desks in this position because it can be quite confronting and draining to be constantly facing someone else. I suggested to my client that she should talk to her staff members and ask them how they would like to have their desks positioned (space permitting). I gave her some ideas of where the desks would be best suited to let the Feng Shui energy flow and also where the staff members could have more privacy and less confronting or aggressive energy.

The second thing that I noticed in the office was that there was no color anywhere, no plants and no pictures or artwork on the walls. There was nothing to make the staff members feel inspired or even to make them feel comfortable or that they belonged in the office.

I suggested to my client that she may like to add some artwork to the walls or some posters, or an indoor plant such as a jade plant or any other indoor plant that has good Feng Shui. By adding artwork or plants to the office it makes the office area feel less clinical and more inviting. The plants also help to bring in positive new energy and they help to clear the air.

Another important thing that I spoke to my client about was the importance of clearing the stagnant energy out of the office on a regular basis. I told my client about using a space clearing spray made up of essential oils, or an oil burner or oil diffuser to help lift the energy in the office and to get rid of any negative or stagnant energy.

The purpose of making some of these changes to the office was to lift the stagnant energy, to create a positive and welcoming work environment. I said to my client if she can make these changes and keep her staff members happy and connect with more often so that they feel like they belong and are part of a team, they are more likely to stay working for her. She understood what I was saying and she told me that she was actually looking forward to creating a new work space and making the office a more productive and positive environment for her and all of her staff.

CHAPTER FIVE

HOW TO SPACE CLEAR YOUR BUSINESS TO SELL IT FAST

FENG SHUI

If you plan to or are trying to sell your business there are some important Feng Shui tips that you can use to help sell it faster. When using the principles of Feng Shui you can easily analyze what does and doesn't make your work place feel inviting, positive and appealing to people.

By using Feng Shui principles you can save yourself stress, time and money because you will be creating a positive energy in and around your work place to welcome in potential buyers for your business.

It is important to realize though that Feng Shui principles alone will not sell your business, there are other important things that you need to have such as a good real estate agent who knows the market well and can create a marketing plan that will draw potential buyers to you as well helping you to find the right price to sell your business for.

There are many things that you can do to clear the energy in your work place as I have written about earlier, here are some additional hints to help you to sell your business fast

Take note of what your work place building looks like from the outside

Imagine that you are a buyer or someone that has never met you or been to your work place before, what do you think your work place looks like from the outside? Remember first impressions last and it only takes a few seconds for a person to judge what they think about the appearance of your work place.

Be honest with what you see, try to take the emotion out of it when you look at your work place. You need to take into account the styles and current trends of the time, what may have been fashionable five to ten years ago may now be outdated and could possibly turn potential buyers off.

Go with the adage less is more, try to steer away from too many bright colors because potential buyers want to be able to see the work place as a blank canvas to which they can then add their own sense of style to make it their own business.

De-clutter your work place

To keep the energy positive in your business try to create a work place that feels spacious. You can do this by removing any excess clutter including extra pieces of furniture, files, boxes or knick knacks.

Potential buyers need to be able to connect with your business and visualize where they will put their own personal belongings. If a work place is full of too many personal items or too much clutter it can be hard for a buyer to connect and feel like their business would belong there.

It is also important that the energy moves freely around the work place. If you have a spare office or room that is full of junk, make sure that you store those items away neatly in boxes or you may even like to store them offsite at a storage facility just while you are in the process of selling your business.

Clean your work place

As simple as it sounds it is extremely important that you clean the whole work place including all of the floors, windows, blinds, shutters and bathrooms. Potential buyers will open drawers and cupboards up to look inside so if possible clean out your drawers and cupboards as well.

When you clean your work place you are attracting in positive new energy, this is a great thing to do when you are selling your business. People can notice the difference in the energy of a work place that is clean and clear and a work place that is tired, dusty and stagnant.

Clear the benchtops in your kitchen, put any excess plates, cups or cutlery away. Try to have a bowl of fresh fruit in your kitchen and/or a healthy indoor plant. If you put a bunch of fresh flowers in a nice vase in your kitchen it will make the room look and smell fantastic.

Pay attention to how your office or work place smells. Use essential oils or scented candles which have soft pleasant scents, you don't want a scent that is too heavy or overpowering.

Intention to sell

Sometimes one owner of a business wants to sell the business but another owner in the business doesn't want to move or sell. It is very important that everyone who owns the business is open to and willing to sell.

If someone doesn't want to move or sell it can actually energetically block the business from being sold. If everyone is clear and positive and releases their attachment to the business it will help the business to sell a lot quicker. Try to focus on and look forward to what the sale of your business will do for you, it will open up new beginnings.

Deities, Gods and Goddesses to Call Upon to Sell your Business

Feng Shui is not the only tool that you can use to help you to sell your business quickly. There are many deities, gods and goddesses which you can call upon or pray to who will help you to move forward in your life so that you can sell your business if you want to.

You don't have to be a religious person or be part of a particular faith to call upon these deities. All you need to do is to have a clear and positive intention about what you want to achieve. You also need to be open and grateful and say thank you to the deities, gods or goddesses when you are working with them.

In Hinduism there are some very helpful gods and goddesses such as the Goddess Lakshmi who brings financial abundance and the Elephant God Ganesh who is the remover of all obstacles. I personally use Ganesh in my everyday life. I take time to think about what obstacles I need to be removed and then I ask Ganesh for help.

When you need to remove any obstacles, say you want to sell your business but it is taking a while, it is a good idea to have a picture of Ganesh on your mobile phone or you can print it out and have it somewhere where you can see it every day.

To ask Ganesh to remove any obstacles you need to ask in your mind or out loud the following request "Ganesh, please remove all obstacles so that I can sell my business quickly to the right person for the right price, for the benefit of all and harm to none. Thank you." I always state for the good of all and harm to none when I pray or ask for help because I do not want anyone to come to harm as a result of my request. If you do this every day and feel very positive and grateful you will notice very quickly some great results. Make sure that you say thank you to any Deity that you call upon.

There are many other gods, goddesses and deities that you can call upon or pray to that can help you with abundance and/or selling your business. It is up to you what feels right and what your particular beliefs are.

Here is a list of gods, goddesses and deities specifically chosen to help you to sell your business:

Abundanta	– Abundance and finances
Ganesh	– Abundance and removing obstacles
Krishna	– Joy and happiness
Lakshmi	– Space clearing, abundance, beauty, manifesting

In the Catholic faith some people pray to St. Joseph to help them to sell their home, you can also use the same prayer to sell your business. There is a specific prayer to St. Joseph and also a St. Joseph Novena. Here is the prayer to St. Joseph to sell a business:

Prayer to St. Joseph to sell a business

O, Saint Joseph, you who taught our Lord the carpenter's trade, and saw to it that he was always properly housed, hear my earnest plea.

I want you to help me now as you helped your foster-child Jesus, and as you have helped many others in the matter of housing.

I wish to sell this business quickly, easily, and profitably and I implore you to grant my wish by bringing me a good buyer, one who is eager, compliant and honest, and by letting nothing impede the rapid conclusion of the sale.

Dear Saint Joseph, I know you would do this for me out of the goodness of your heart and in your own good time, but my need is very great now and so I must make you hurry on my behalf.

*Saint Joseph, I am going to place you in a difficult position
with your head in darkness and you will suffer as our Lord
suffered, until this business is sold. Then, Saint Joseph,
I swear before the cross and God Almighty, that I will redeem
you and you will receive my gratitude and a place of honor
in my home.*

Amen.

The St. Joseph Novena is a prayer which people say for
nine days in a row, each day has a different prayer. Many
people say the St. Joseph Novena to pray for what they want
specifically, so if you want to sell your business you should
have that thought in your mind and really focus upon it and
mean it while you say the Novena.

The St. Joseph Novena

*Day one: Oh God, guide of those who listen and helper of
those who hear your voice, speak to me, as you did to St.
Joseph, and help me accomplish the things you give me to do.*

*Day two: O God, you love your people and bless the ordinary
lives we quietly live. As you blessed St. Joseph, bless what I
do, however hidden and simple it may be, and let all I do be
done with love.*

*Day three: O God, ever faithful, you remember us always and
in time reveal your blessings. Help me trust in you, as St.
Joseph faithfully trusted, and never let me lose faith in the
wonderful gifts you promise me.*

Day four: God of families, bless the family that's mine. Keep us safe from harm, and never let evil come between us. Let peace remain in our hearts.

Day five: O God, who loves children, be kind to our children today. Give them eyes of faith for seeing far, a loving heart for welcoming life, and a place always at your side.

Day six: God of our heavenly home, bless our home on earth. Let the spirit of Mary and Joseph rest at our table, shape our words and actions, and bring blessing to our children.

Day seven: God, our Father, give your fatherly spirit to those who are fathers now. Like Joseph, give them hearts of devoted love for their wives and children and strength for forgiveness and patience.

Day eight: Give shelter, O God, to those who need it, and bring together families divided. Give us enough to eat, and decent work to earn our bread. Care for us, O God.

Day nine: Bless all families, O Lord especially those in need. Remembering the life of your Son, we pray for the poor, for those who lack a good home, for those in exile. Grant them a protector like Joseph, O God.

Amen.

Some people also believe that it is very helpful to put a St. Joseph medal or statue in the letterbox of the business that they want to sell. Other people believe in burying a St. Joseph statue upside down in the yard of the business that they want to sell as well as saying the St. Joseph prayer or novena.

Each person has their own belief systems so what feels right for some people may not feel right for another person. Stick to what feels right for you, there is no right or wrong way to do things, you may be drawn to a particular deity or you may prefer to focus on manifesting what you want without the deity.

VISION BOARDS

A vision board is a wonderful way for you to focus on what you want to achieve, it is very a very important tool for success because it helps you to remain positive and focused. The positive focused intent helps you to use the law of attraction to attract in what you want.

A vision board is a piece of paper, cardboard or a piece of board where you can make a visual collage of what you want to achieve or attract into your life. Vision boards give you clarity about what it is you want or desire. When you make a vision board you are putting your intent and emotion into it.

You can make your vision board quite simply by writing words on a piece of paper or you may like to create a collage and/or draw pictures, put photos on the board or cut pictures out of a magazine to stick on the board.

Vision boards make you focus on images and words. When you focus on your vision board you start to manifest and attract in what you want. Because vision boards are used to attract in what you want in life it is important that you be very specific about what it is that you want to attract in. For example if you want to sell your business quickly and for the right price, you can take a photo of your business logo or your businesses location and place it on your vision board. You can then write sold across the photo and put a date you want it sold by and a price that you want to sell it for. You may even like to write a statement such as "My business will sell for ___ by this date _____, this sale will go through smoothly. Both myself and the new owners will be very happy with the outcome of the sale."

A vision board is a very personal thing it is totally up to you what you put on it, it is also up to you whether you hide it in a cupboard or drawer or if you tell anyone about it. Usually you would have the vision board on display where you can see it every day so you can focus upon it.

Remember the most important thing about a vision board is the intent behind it, focus on what you want to achieve and remain positive.

25 Years... It's Time To Sell!

I had a client come to see me who wanted to sell his business. He had owned the business for over 25 years and he was looking at retiring. He wanted to have time to enjoy being able to travel with his wife while they were still young and healthy enough to enjoy it.

The problem was that he had already had his business up for sale for over six months and there hadn't been any interest or any offers. This was causing him and his wife a lot of stress and frustration. They couldn't understand why there was no one interested in buying their business when it was a very profitable business with many regular customers.

The reason this client had come to see me was to see if there was anything that he could do to sell his business faster for the price that he wanted. When I tuned in and looked into this clients business psychically, I could see a big black shadow over the business. It felt like there was an umbrella overshadowing it. I also felt that his business couldn't even be seen online for sale, the pictures I saw in my mind were very dark and didn't look appealing at all.

I mentioned all of this information to my client, he said that it all makes sense to him because he and his agent hadn't had any enquiries online at all about the business being for sale. He also said that there were big trees out the front of his office building which block the view of the building from the street. These trees were very overgrown and the lighting outside the building was very poor.

I suggested to him that he needed to get better lighting outside the front of the building, he also need to maintain and trim the front trees so that the office building is visible and more attractive to potential buyers.

Another suggestion that I made was that he should have new photos taken after making these changes so that there is more light in the photos and the photos should be better quality photos which show a bright, well-organized office space to highlight how great his business is. My client understood everything that I suggested and he said he would definitely try to make these changes as soon as possible.

I also said to my client that he had to make sure that he was 100 percent ready to hand his business over to someone else. He explained to me that at first he was worried about selling because he was so attached to the business and he was worried that someone else may not look after his loyal customers properly. He then went on to say that after waiting for so long for the business to sell he was now ready to sell and was detached from the emotional connection with the business. He just wanted it to sell to the right person.

When I heard my client say that he is ready to sell, I asked him if he had ever heard of the Hindu Elephant God Ganesh, he replied that he hadn't heard of him. So I explained how to call upon Ganesh to remove any obstacles in your life, and I explained he is especially helpful when you want to remove obstacles to help sell real estate.

My client said he was looking forward to putting all of these things into place and he would get back to me if he had any success in selling his business. About one or two months later I did hear from this client and he was happy to tell me that he finally had a contract to sell his business and he was looking forward to going on a holiday with his wife. It just goes to show you how important it is to have good Feng Shui in your work place and to also have the right intent when you are wanting to sell your business.